SCHOOLS OF TOMORROW

RICHARD NORTH

Schools
of Tomorrow

Education As If People Matter

GREEN BOOKS

First published by
Green Books
Hartland
Bideford
Devon EX39 6EE

British Library Cataloguing in Publication Data
North, Richard
Schools of tomorrow: education as if people matter
1. Progressive education
I. Title
371' . 04 LA126

ISBN 1–870098–06–4

Typeset by Type Matters
15 Devon Square, Newton Abbot, Devon
Printed by Robert Hartnoll (1985) Ltd
Victoria Square, Bodmin, Cornwall

Contents

Preface by L. C. Taylor

CHAPTER ONE
   Introduction   1

CHAPTER TWO
   Competing Images of School   9

CHAPTER THREE
   The Hartland Model   25

CHAPTER FOUR
   The Lewknor Model   47

CHAPTER FIVE
   The Danish Model   59

CHAPTER SIX
   The Issue of Size   71

CHAPTER SEVEN
   The Research   85

CHAPTER EIGHT
   The New Style of Education   99

CHAPTER NINE
   The Political Environment   113

Appendix 1—Ten Beauty Tips For Small Schools   131

Appendix 2—Manifesto: Movement For Education
   on a Human Scale   141

Suggested Reading   148

Useful Addresses   149

The publishers would like to acknowledge, with grateful thanks, the assistance of the following organisations in the publication of this book:

The G & H Roberts Community Trust, Scotland.

The Calouste Gulbenkian Foundation, London.

— not, of course, for the base reasons of economy some unworthily suspected, but for the good of the children. In the circular, criteria were issued about square-footage per child for assembly space, playgrounds and the rest which the small village schools cannot meet, and bureaucratic heads were sadly shaken about the effect of insufficient specialist skills available in the one- or two-teacher school. All this as if a village school, in fact as in law, is an entity separate from its surrounding village. It must be a rare village school that fails to make regular use of the village hall, the recreation ground and the surrounding fields, and of the skills of adults living in the village, to provide a more generous space and a richer diet than can any school relying on its own resources. At the time of the new regulations, an international survey by O.E.C.D. of 'Basic schooling and teacher support in sparsely-populated areas' collected evidence about how small schools, both primary and lower secondary, could be effectively run. It showed how countries had worked with ingenuity and determination to preserve schools much smaller than any we have in Britain, and revealed no other country that shared the British obsession with wholesale closure. At last, a month before the recent election, announcements were made by the new Secretary of State, Mr Kenneth Baker, which seemed to rescind the early bit of nonsense about primary schools. The D.E.S. in its revision didn't actually *say very much* (each case is to be considered on its merits — as always), but press and public have seen it as an amber light against closures by the L.E.A.s, who had a green, green light from the D.E.S. before.

If, just before the election, the Secretary of State seemed to grant remission to small primary schools, the realisation that he may also have signalled a change affecting small secondary schools emerged only during the election. When comprehensive schooling was officially promulgated in the celebrated Circular 144 (1947), the approved ideal at secondary level was the large, all-true comprehensive school

Preface

L.C. Taylor

RICHARD NORTH has written this brief vigorous book as part of a campaign which aims to apply to education the philosophy of Fritz Schumacher. 'Small is beautiful', the title of Schumacher's most famous book, has become a popular aphorism: for 'big' is too often in-appropriate, impersonal, boring and bureaucratic. The sub-title of that book was 'A study of economics as if people matter'. In similar vein, the sub-title of Richard North's book is 'Education as if people matter'.

The campaign aims to support smallness in several contexts: at the primary level, by helping local parents resist the closure of village schools; at the secondary level, by arguing for the retention of smaller L.E.A. schools (threatened more than ever because their numbers fall with the declining birthrate), by promoting the practices of some large comprehensives which are trying to create smaller 'schools' within the large school, and by urging the value of creating new, small secondary schools; support too, for those parents who, from a wide range of motives, use the residual right allowed in the 1944 Education Act to provide 'education otherwise' in that smallest of schools, the family home.

Discussions towards launching the Campaign for Education on a Human Scale began in the autumn of 1985. The date should be noted. It long preceded the extraordinary proposals in the Conservative manifesto which suddenly made education a major election issue. When the Campaign began effects were being felt of damaging regulations on school premises (1981) issued by the Department of Education and Science under Sir Keith Joseph. These had the effect of accelerating the closure of small village schools

Photographs

Chapter One
Pupils Participate in the Discussion of their School Affairs, The Small School, Hartland, Maureen Mellor, Devon Life.

Chapter Two
Lunch is a Shared Activity, The Small School, Hartland, Maureen Mellor, Devon Life.

Chapter Three
Hometime, The Small School, Hartland, David Rose, The Independent.

Chapter Four
A Practical Beginning, Leuknor School, Oxford.

Chapter Five
Independent Learning at a Danish Small School.

Chapter Six
Life in a Twig, The Small School, Hartland, Maureen Mellor, Devon Life.

Chapter Seven
Experiments in a Small Lab, The Small School, Hartland, Maureen Mellor, Devon Life.

Chapter Eight
Education for Capability at Warlingham Park School, Croydon.

Chapter Nine
Learning by Doing, The Small School, Hartland, Maureen Mellor, Devon Life.

(then recommended as having a *minimum* of 10 streams or 1600 children "to ensure a viable and economic sixth form"). Since then lack of resources for wholesale rebuilding and some doubts about the effect of size have resulted, in practice, in the acceptance of some scaling down: now it seems there may be, in principle as well, some welcome within the state-supported educational system for something much smaller. The Conservative Party during the election presaged that schools that do not charge fees (an astute dividing line), nor suddenly become academically selective in their entry if they were not before, may apply for 'grant-maintained' status. If accepted, they will receive direct from the D.E.S. an amount per child equivalent to the amount paid by central government to the L.E.A.s (about £2000 a year at present). The new arrangement may well rescue many smaller state schools at present threatened with closure or amalgamation.

During the recent election it happened that grant-maintained status was argued about solely in terms of existing state schools opting out of L.E.A. control, but presumably that was only part of what was intended. For unless the system of schools in Britain is to be frozen into Byzantine immobility the same principle should presumably apply, in time, to existing schools outside the state system which renounce the charging of fees, to new schools founded on a non-fee-paying basis, and conceivably to parents who elect to educate their own children at home. To take some actual examples: by what determining principle would the D.E.S. reject an application for grant-maintained status from, say, existing or newly-created Rudolf Steiner day schools? Such schools charge minimal fees, which they might be willing to renounce, are non-selective in academic terms, and would strike most adults as educationally admirable — always excepting those who judge by the grandeur of buildings and the elaboration of equipment. And will the only new schools to be recognised for grant-maintained status be the Government's own city technology colleges? If so, it seems that industrialists alone are to be favoured as founding fathers — a very odd contraction of educational values, most un-Victorian, curiously exclusive. And what about the 600 parents who belong to associations like Education Otherwise, or The Parents' New Educational Union (P.N.E.U.)? These associations support home education, which has to be certified as satisfactory, home by home, by the L.E.A. Although more common for children below 11 than for those between 11 and 16, the popularity of home education at the lower secondary stage might rapidly increase if some official support were now to be given. During the election, the Government's opponents accused it simply of wanting to revive selective schools and to release a few schools from the invasive social engineering of some Far Left L.E.A.s: its supporters claimed such motives as the right of parents to have real choice among schools, and real influence within the school. Such ideas would prove radical indeed. For too long in Britain parental choice in schooling has been confined to two unsatisfactory extremes — accepting, like it or lump it, what the state provides, wholly free, or opting for private education and paying the full cost, year upon expensive year — a fictional alternative for most. Other countries manage better. For example, in (then Socialist) Denmark (as described in this book), in Holland, Canada and elsewhere, secondary schools can be started by a variety of organisations or by parents getting together. Working within the framework of a national curriculum, such schools can qualify for substantial state support, so that they become affordable by a wide range of people. Can it really be true that this Conservative Government intends some comparable freedom for us?

This possibility, added to a widespread disillusion with large schools, makes a Campaign for Education on a Human Scale especially timely. Most of the existing, non-posh, less elaborate private secondary schools — those which might

prefer to receive a central grant rather than to charge fees —
are in practice small; new schools are certain to start small
and many will remain so. It is one of the merits of Richard
North in this book, however, that he does not claim
smallness as a panacaea; still less does he try, on the basis of
research, to prove it so. Smallness certainly makes many
desirable qualities in a school more likely, but bigness
favours others. As for the available research about the effects
of size it points, of course, every which way. The point is that
many parents put smallness high in their priorities, or would
if they had the chance. Education is a nebulous, complex,
individual, uncertain matter (by comparison with which an
eminent American scientist referred to "the simplicities of
landing a man on the moon"). Because education has so many
aims, many of them conflicting, and because reasonable
individuals differ about what weight should be given to
different aims, no-one can say what is 'best', still less how to
achieve it. Best for which particular young person, from what
sort of home, and with what sort of parents or parent? Best
now — or in the long term? Principally with a view to
employability or to a 'preparation for life'? For what sort of
'life' — one we consider likely, the rusty world being what it
is, or one we aspire to — reflecting what moral imperatives or
what religious beliefs? So on and on the educational debate
continues, unavoidably couched in clichés and half-truths
that haven't changed in essentials since the pyramids were
built.

For ultimately views about education are a matter of
values. The key question is: given so many justifiable
alternatives, who principally should decide between them?
Much the same sort of state school can be provided for
everyone: alternatively, a greater variety of schools, different
in significant ways, can be provided by many different bodies
for parents with their children to choose among. In Britain in
the last forty years the tendency has been toward uniformity:
elsewhere diversity has been preferred. The reasons are more

fundamental than politics. In Britain, in education as in most walks of life, it is the producers, organised in powerful professional associations and in unions, who dominate and direct. The state provides a system reflecting, as far as resources permit, a consensus of professionals' views — in this case, teachers' and administrators'. In other Western countries the state deliberately reinforces the *consumer* interest, and in education the result is greater variety, often less expensive elaboration in specialist facilities and, between schools and in many details within schools, a greater say for parents. It is some such extension in parental choice that Richard North urges. That implies increasing the number and sorts of schools for parents to choose among — more and various (which means that many will be small) rather than few and large, uniform in many essentials because of the pressures of size and of their direct administration by the local authority. When the Campaign for Education on a Human Scale was launched, when this book was begun, such views simply bucked the system. Who could have forseen that such a cause would become consonant, in principle at least, with a sudden transformation with (as it happens) Conservative educational policy? Will their election rhetoric about parent power, parent choice and variety in schools, together with their general emphasis on individual initiative, small business and reduction of public monopolies, now be reflected in the imminent Education Bill? Will a principle argued solely in the context of established schools opting out extend to a more likely source of recruitment, a lively prospect for educational change — newly-founded schools opting in? That remains to be seen — and vigorously to be campaigned for.   June 1987

L.C. (Kim) Taylor was headmaster of Sevenoaks School for fourteen years, then Director of the Nuffield Foundation's project on 'Resources for Learning', from which he wrote the Penguin volume with the same title. Subsequently, as a principle administrator at the O.E.C.D. in Paris, he directed various European and international projects, especially those connected with educational development in rural and remote places. He was then appointed Head of Educational Programme Services at the Independent Broadcasting Authority. He is currently Director of the Calouste Gulbenkian Foundation in London.

CHAPTER ONE
Introduction

Introduction

"KENNETH BAKER'S new circular on the school system, released in early May, 1987, has brought little comfort to Lewknor School, at the picturesque village of that name in Oxfordshire.

"Though the new document removed some of the specific suggestions on the size below which schools cannot be efficient which were contained in the draft, it leaves in place much of the conventional wisdom that is prejudiced against small schools.

"For the last fifteen years, under the headmastership of Mervyn Benford, Lewknor has become a model of the adventurous solutions a forty- or fifty-pupil primary school can find to the inherent difficulties of providing a full range of subjects in a small school.

"They involved breaking down some of the distinctions between subjects in the curriculum, and also in the rigid practice of banding children either by age or ability.

"At Lewknor, a child will sometimes be in a class with the full range of ages in the school learning from each other, and sometimes in groups where the level of knowledge is assumed to be roughly similar.

"But one of the most daring innovations was to seek

funding for a third teacher from a range of sources including foundations, companies and the local community.

"The local education authority, Oxfordshire County Council, said that it will not continue to allow Lewknor's funding of this teacher, on the grounds that it accords unequal treatment to the school. Its move may effectively block the project.

"Jill Hudson, the school's new headmistress, says that her village is not particularly affluent. 'Other schools raise money for televisions and cassette recorders: we wanted a teacher,' she says.

"Brian Day, the Deputy Chief Education Officer for Oxfordshire notes that part of the reason why the circular will make little difference in practice is that Oxfordshire always did take each case on its merits.

" 'We have three small school closures with the Secretary of State for consideration. The education committee has just undertaken a review of 85 schools, which is all but completed, and I don't believe that this council will consider any more closures until 1989.'

"Lewknor's former headmaster, Mr Benford, is now co-ordinating an Oxfordshire project which seeks to 'cluster' small schools together so that they can offer a wider range of educational opportunities to their pupils. The project is mirrored by many counties with many small schools, as they try to discover means to deliver an education of the 'necessary breadth, balance, relevance and differentiation' which the government rightly requires of them."

That was, very roughly, a news story I wrote for *The Independent* last Spring. The news story illustrates the sort of thinking in local authorities which might drive a school to go independent. It was swiftly followed by news that Kenneth Baker was heading into the election with a plan that schools should be able to opt out of the local education authority (L.E.A.) network and umbrella, and instead form a trust of parents and locals and teachers and become directly responsible to the State's Department of Education and Science instead.

There followed light debate on whether this was an election winner or not (though there was very little doubt that it was intended to be so). Some, especially left-wingers, felt that this was a charter for the return to grammar schools by the back door. The assumption was that the good schools might be tempted to go down this route; but that the bad ones, with all their problems, would remain inside the present framework.

For my part, I welcomed the move because whether it is wholly good or bad, it opens the way to educational diversity. However, there is still, hovering in the background, the Government's (I mean the Tory Government of May, 1987) idea that there should be a national curriculum. In other words, the State still is seen as knowing what children should learn, even if the Government felt that a certain administrative independence might be popular and useful.

I concede all the difficulties of ensuring that there is not a flight toward the better schools by anyone with nerve and skill, and perhaps education credits from the Government, whilst poor schools in poor neighbourhoods suffer a concentration of problems and are overwhelmed. Because educational success and failure is more to do with the spirit than with cash, I doubt these problems are insuperable. But that is not the entire point. This is a book about how inadequately muscular are our ideas about what children need to learn and how feeble and yet constricting are the institutions in which they are taught.

Too many children have had their lives blighted, at least temporarily and perhaps permanently, by lousy education, mostly brought on by an endemic passivity in the relation between the customers (parents and children) and the providers of school (teachers and education authorities).

This, then, is an attempt to describe a new way of looking at the teaching of children. I especially hope that it will not alienate people of the Left merely because it was a minister of the (wet) Right who first looked likely to undo some of the restrictive structures which stand betweeen parents and children achieving the sort of schooling outlined here.

But what is the schooling I want? It is neither free of scholasticism, nor of painting, nor of good practical skills. It does not spurn excellence, nor expect massive achievement of every child. It is to do with making children feel that they have the means of achieving the goals they set themselves: that they know their way around their own culture and their own minds and skills.

It is a question in part of breaking down the worlds of work and leisure: I think the world is moving toward a way of achieving many things, from the servicing of a car to an education for a child, in which it is possible that people will have been led into a way of thinking where they can hardly remember whether they are being paid for what they do or not. In other words, that 'adding value' may be attached to looking after a person for no money as well as to shunting a little currency across some percentage difference revealed on a television screen.

I think ideally that education will not necessarily take place in school at all. I think that it almost certainly will have to be freed from the tyranny of teachers, and that teachers need to be freed from parroting out last year's lessons.

I hope readers will accept that these ideas are offered modestly.

CHAPTER TWO

Competing Images Of School

Competing Images Of School

SCHOOLS ARE big news at the moment, and big politics, too. They are a natural subject for dissension. Education costs us all dearly in taxation; but that is the least of our concerns about it. We all went to school, after all, and carry around with us profound prejudices about what we learned, or did not learn there.

What happens to our children at school will have a major effect on whether they 'do well' and are happy later on. Whether our children are well served at school will largely determine how this nation does; and from that consideration flows both the social well-being of our wider home, and the likely flow of funds for our state pensions.

Put crudely, there is evidence that plenty of children are failed by school. We always have the failure of the present system ringing in our ears. Getting on for half the children in Britain's schools leave without an examination certificate. Our education system remains extraordinarily skewed in favour of preparing all children as though they were potential candidates for Oxford and Cambridge, with a syllabus which is intellectual and not practical; theoretical rather than goal-oriented; and schematic rather than dedicated to providing children with skills.

The Government's own White Paper, *Better Schools,*

(H.M.S.O., Command 9469, 1985) spells out a record of considerable failure considering that it speaks of a system which consumes up to £2,000 per pupil per year. It speaks of a considerable mismatch between pupils' needs and abilities and what they are taught, and of a teaching system which depends far too much on teachers closely directing the work of young people.

It is true that 27 per cent of children (including those that come through the independent system) manage to get the equivalent of 5 'O' Levels and that 17 per cent manage an 'A' Level. Yet there is serious doubt that these are good results for a system dedicated to obtaining that sort of achievement, nor that it is a sufficiently worthwhile result to have risked wasting an enormous amount of time, energy and opportunity obtaining it.

And of course schools are, we believe, mirror images of the various forces pulling this society about. Whether we see our children go off to be taught in an open-plan, relaxed, free-for-all, where anti-racism and anti-sexism and patois are all the rage, or to a sit-up-straight sort of place, where the day begins with prayer and is spent facing the front and learning how to parse sentences, will — inevitably — colour what we think about school and the schooling process.

Schools are, inevitably, one of the battlegrounds where ideologues most like to conduct their struggle. There will be ideologues of the Left, too subtle to believe that Marx should be read to children at lunchtime, but not averse to slipping in a little subliminal information about the foul deeds of colonialists or large corporations, and mad keen on taking children on demos to support teachers against 'Maggie's cuts'.

And there will be ideologues of the Right, keen to stress that English is a single language, and that in its standard form it is a passport to success for all comers, and keen to teach the merits of competition, whether in tests or on the football field.

Everyone knows these sorts of distinctions. We see them in headlines, as when a 'progressive' headmistress comes up against her 'reactionary' parents, or when a 'reactionary' headmaster suggests that positive discrimination will damage the 'indigenous' population, and probably the immigrant population too. We hear of schools where the local Anglican vicar has been barred from giving a little religious instruction in school (to the outrage of the Hindu and Moslem parents, who like a God-centred world). We hear of L.E.A.s which dislike seeing policemen in schools, fearing that policemen are not nice people.

We hear of schools which are rough-houses, and where teachers are profoundly dispirited. Down the road, we hear of a tolerably happy sort of school, with a student population drawn from the same neighbourhood and social background. And of poor standards in reading, writing and arithmetic, with fierce letters to the papers denouncing declining standards.

But on inspection, behind the horror stories, which are mostly inflated but not always, we find the normal curate's egg.

It seems that many schools are pretty orderly, and that many are very dull. We find that standards are not all that low, either compared with schooling abroad or schooling as it used to be done here. We find that there is rather little to celebrate or be joyous about. Indeed, perhaps the most obvious ground for complaint is that for every plainly lousy education someone receives or takes from the system, there are oceans of tedium and under-achievement.

But beware the person who believes he or she has the answer.

It seems to be the case that schooling is like stock-manship on a farm. There is a strong desire to find a systematic way of teaching children, just as there is in the art of getting lots of good beef from a herd of cattle. But in the end, the evidence suggests that no one of the most

prized and cherished shibboleths of particular individuals
will serve.

Big classes, small classes; creative thinking versus rote
learning; mixed-ability classes or strict streaming; none of
these alone will do the trick.

Educational theorists have their arguments, and they
commission or undertake bits of research, which are
probably more or less worth doing. But one finds no
answers come from any of them. At least, no answers which
make it clear that if one did this or that, and pursued this or
that policy, one would get a predictable result.

The enterprise is just too human for that.

This does not mean that expertise is not involved in
running a school. It is. A new head can make or wreck a
school within a few weeks of taking up an appointment.
Further down, the rot takes longer, but is just as sure. What
makes a good school, that basket of qualities which will flow
from a chemistry which is infinitely subtle, robust, peculiar
and unpredictable, will not flow from any particular theory,
though it often flows from one person, or a small group of
people, who are in the grip of some theory or other.

There are two certainties. Running a good school is
extraordinarily difficult and demanding (though it may be
intuitive). And no-one holds a monopoly on the means by
which a good school may be achieved.

These two truths require of anyone who suggests a
reform to the system a very particular modesty. However
good the ideas behind the proposed reform (and however
bad), in the end, they will be turned into a good school by a
process much more problematic than the business of having
a good or true idea. They will become a good school only if
they can be married to people of sufficient stability,
resilience, passion, dedication and fairness to be the heart
and soul of an institution which must deal with the human
spirit and mind.

The second truth requires a modesty on the part of the

custodians of the system as it now is. This is that they have not the smallest right to claim any solid evidence for whichever theory they espouse, nor any theoretical right to suppose that the next person to come along with an idea for schools has not at last hit on something rather sound.

This is a small book about education, and it was commissioned by the Schumacher Society, which believes that 'small is beautiful'. In particular, this book flows from the work of Satish Kumar and his friends and colleagues who run the Small School in Hartland, Devon.

Because it is a school like most others, with some bright and interesting children in it, and because — like some but not all schools — it has some exceptional teachers, it will almost certainly turn out some exceptional characters. But I do not think that makes a good argument for small schools.

Indeed, I can think of some very good reasons to worry about small schools. The most obvious is that they will be parochial, and dominated by one or two teachers. Another is that they may find it hard to arrange sufficient contact between pupils and a wide range of adult intellects. Some argue they will find competitive sports hard to arrange. We will come to other objections, and deal with them.

But what matters tremendously, I think, is that some educators who happen to prefer large schools for practical and administrative reasons are trying to peddle arguments about small schools which are simply patently untrue. These arguments depend on some theoretical ideas and on some bits of evidence which just do not work.

The evidence has nothing to say about the quality of small schools, any more than it does on big schools. There simply is no evidence that a big school or a small school will turn out children with this or that quality. The coolest and most reasoned accounts I have read of small schools say that one can measure no educational difference between pupils who have spent years in them as against those who have gone to big schools.

It remains the case that I have no intention of sending my children to a big school if I can find a good small one. I have a prejudice in favour of smallness, and am prepared to sacrifice other things for it. You may not be prepared to make the same sacrifice, and your children may be all the better off for it.

Actually, the lack of evidence either way about whether smallness or bigness — just as the lack of evidence on many other educational theories — leaves parents in a very powerful position when they argue that what they like — as simple as that, what they *want* — should be an important consideration for educational authorities. Parents are doing the paying; they are raising the pupils and have to live, long-term, with the results of success or failure.

Of course, as Mary Warnock pointed out in her Dimbleby lecture a couple of years back, the teacher and not the parent is the specialist in teaching: teachers should be listened to when they talk about what they spend all day doing. Besides, as Warnock also pointed out, schools are institutions, and have a life independent of any parents and teachers. They should not be subjected to casual fashion. On the other hand, she also suggested that teachers should see themselves, and make themselves, a very self-critical professional elite.

However, it is important to note that bringing children to adulthood does not require schools or teachers. There are all sorts of learning in the world, all sorts of skills and aptitudes and disciplines which have been learned in the past and will be learned in the future with no need of schools. Indeed, at this moment schools exist because by a curious mixture of circumstances, parents are mostly out at work, and thus not free to be teaching children — whether their own or their neighbours' — whilst over the years they have been robbed of the confidence that they could teach children.

There are perhaps 2000 families who educate their children at home at the moment. Many of them do a rather good job, and some have, for instance, got their children — or helped them — into university without the aid of teachers. It is important that these people should be funded to club together for mutual support. And they need new institutions they can visit or use to get hold of facilities they cannot provide at home. The fact that they are educating their children needs to be recognised, and to be funded.

The teacher is likely to be the greatest obstacle to a good educational system in the future. This is not to say that there are not plenty of men and women teachers who have been and will continue to be an inspiration to the young people they teach. It is only to say that an idea has grown up in the minds of most teachers that it is they that do and should educate children.

This makes them the natural enemies of a different view of education which suggests that children should learn for themselves, so far as possible. Parents, other children, the television, radio, books, experimentation, computers, should all be more important to children as educators than teachers. Crucially, and we have much to do in this area, children should be learning from 'extension learning' tools, in schools, or at home, in much the way that adults are using the National Extension College or the Open University.

As L.C. (Kim) Taylor pointed out in his book *'Resources for Learning'* in 1971, the most important change in the quality of schooling from a child's point of view occurs when teachers cut right back on the amount of 'teaching'. The very word 'teacher' conjures up an adult pouring out words to a whole class of children lined up in desks ("like figures in a sum," said Dickens) being taken through the same course at the same pace — or as near to it as they can manage. It is because verbal 'teaching' is still regarded as central — whatever occasional variants there may be — that schools try to have lots of specialists (and how the number of specialisms multiplies — the wider the curriculum the more there are), and each of these specialists wants more and more specialised facilities and equipment, and urges 'streaming' into sets and classes as homogeneous as possible, so that most of those present can follow the spiel at the level the teacher pitches it. Then enough children have to be collected from near and far to make the whole enterprise workable and economic. That's why the comprehensive secondary schools, especially those like ours run on American high school lines with a smorgasbord curriculum, tend to grow so large. Whenever a more independent style of learning is deliberately made central (what Taylor called 'resource-based learning', and is sometimes called nowadays 'supported self-study') a major transformation occurs. He cites many examples, such as P.N.E.U. in Britain, the Dalton Plan in America, the Freinet system in France, each of them widespread and successful at one time and still continuing. An important incidental benefit from a real break with the assumption that the main way to learn is from the lips of a (preferably specialist) teacher is that much smaller secondary schools become more workable, and so does home education.

Teachers can encourage, discipline, lead, order and manage the education of children; but the teaching must be done by the child in contact with writers, doers, musicians, mechanics, nurses. Importantly, of course, the child should be taught by parents, friends, neighbours. The monopolisation of education by teachers is the core of what almost all educational reform needs to be about. Later, we will look at the curriculum-led school. And then at the class-led school. The curriculum is the idea of the world of knowledge being divided into subjects; the class the idea of children being grouped together, normally according to age or ability. Both these arrangements, first of the body of knowledge and then the body of learners, arise because of the perceived and historic need to so order a school that a teacher can stand in front of a class and lecture to it.

However much the researchers and commentators bewail the fact that most children, most of the time, are brought up in a crippling dependence upon a teacher, and this can happen as much in a small as in a large school, the fundamental assumption that education is a matter of dividing knowledge into curricula and students into classes persists. To many in the professional educational establishment, improvement depends on trying to loosen the child's dependence on the teacher, but without, it seems, providing him or her with the tools of independence, which should crucially be access to outside stimuli.

To manage the curriculum, the class and the teacher, there has been a relentless economic pressure to have bigger schools. Occasionally, there have been pockets of small schools, especially in the country. But even in these, though the atmosphere is often happy and familial (and thank goodnesss for that), the learning tends to remain teacher-centred, and the agonies of how to achieve a peer-group, and how to deliver a curriculum, remain.

Indeed, the means by which a small school might be made a good place in which to learn as well as a good place in which to live are much the same as those by which education in a large school could be made happier as well as more effective. The large school can be divided into houses easily, and made to feel like a small one. But the educational revolution now needed in most small schools and almost everywhere in big ones is quite separate from the smallness it allows.

Once children were freed from teachers, they could be freed from curricula and classes. They could of course also be freed from schools. But it is likely to remain the case, rather sadly, that schools are convenient marshalling yards for children. Our job now is to ensure that the school becomes as good a place as, say, the home or the library or the factory might be, in which children can learn. This may require independent and small schools not because these are the only places where children can learn freed from teachers, but because the venture will begin experimentally, and thus in a small way, and probably independent of the main educational establishment. But it will also be the case that when learning is freed from teachers, classes and curricula, the main impediment to small schools, which is economic, will be removed. Then their inherent advantages of friendliness and humanness of scale will blossom.

The urge to largeness in schools in the 1960s was something which came from the educational administrators rather than from the teachers or the parents. It chimed well with ideas of the economies of scale which were very fashionable then, and it also chimed well with some ideas about equality of opportunity which now seem a little half-baked to many people (including some egalitarians).

But the rebellion against some of the educational ideas of the sixties and seventies is now deeply entrenched amongst many parents and it may well soon become undeniable. This is simply because there is a strong move across two or three generations of parents and across all income groups for a toughening up of standards in society and schools.

The easy-going sixties and the confused seventies have given way to the rather severe eighties.

And yet, certain changes have been achieved and will endure. The generation of parents which now dominates Western society has lived through the 'Beatle revolution', and was both converted by parts of it and disillusioned by others. It now seems to want certain reliable touchstones returned to social life. Appalled by the decline in 'street' behaviour, and alarmed by unemployment, many modern parents want to try to attempt a new reconciliation between the achievement of excellence and the egalitarianism they learned in the last two or three decades. They have a high regard for the autonomy of each individual, for creativity, for freedom. They want all these reconciled, and it will prove a difficult task.

It hardly matters that the political parties are having some difficulty catching this mood, because the thrusts of society are not coming from them anyway, and perhaps never did. It hardly matters that the ideas of Left and Right do not easily adapt to the new mood. The problems of modern society do not readily yield themselves to an analysis which was always faulty but which served much better when the class system worked fairly well as an analytical tool.

But it does matter a great deal that the new ideas are having some difficulty being met by the school system. Or rather, that the school system is at its weakest when it has to deal with these new strands of thought.

Putting them very roughly, we want to reconcile creativity, competitiveness and co-operation. We are very concerned these days that people should be creative; we are concerned that they should be equipped to master both technological and human goals; we are concerned to allow or develop the entrepreneurial in as many people as possible but that this should be in harmony with the need also to develop the compassionate in them, or at least in society as a whole. We are well aware that discipline is necessary, but that autonomous discipline is better than discipline by rote.

In learning, we want to reconcile the mastery of set skills and the accumulation of data with the excitement of curiosity and the ability to achieve goals. We are concerned that people should love the culture of the past, and know it, whilst being able to be daring enough to be amongst those who make the culture of tomorrow.

Yet the truth is we have no idea what it is the children of the future will need to know and be capable of. We suspect, as a matter of prejudice, that a sound moral sense has always and will always come in handy, and that we have some sort of idea of what that requires of us as we talk to children.

But we have no idea, actually, what we should teach them in terms of their intellectual development. This is a much more profound challenge — a challenge of intention — than has been faced by previous generations dealing with the education of their children.

We know that certain ideas which have been a commonplace for nearly a hundred years have taken a terrible beating of late. One is that the Welfare State should deliver services *in kind* to all disadvantaged people. Another is that most people will be employed by someone else for most of their lives. Another is that science and art are profoundly different things and require different people to pursue them. Another is that to be in business is essentially exploitative rather than creative. Another is that men have only a small role in the bringing up of their children.

We want to find a way of educating our children which combines a decent respect for the past with a practical and intellectual equipment for the present and future.

This uncertainty as to basic purpose further encourages the idea that schools are not necessary institutions. With many other people, I think they may disappear altogether or become places where certain services and resources are offered to people of all ages. This shift of emphasis will quite possibly mean that the teaching profession will disappear, to be replaced by the mechanic-who-teaches-a-bit, or the bank-manager-who-teaches-a-bit, or the nurse-who-teaches-a-bit.

Already we find that there are several thousand parents in this country who do not send their children to school. They are being very brave, in the sense that they get no support from the education system, and sometimes quite active opposition from it. They also face the hazard of being few in number: their children endure being rarities.

However, they make a better model of what to do with

schools than might be supposed. The parent with a child at home has to master the business of teaching without a teacher being there. There could hardly be a more striking case of schooling which gets beyond teachers.

In the last chapter, we look at some of the possibilities for moving the education system on so that it allows or encourages schools in which children are encouraged to learn for themselves. On the way, we look at one or two schools which have moved furthest toward the kind of education which might serve us well, and at some of the prejudices against them.

CHAPTER THREE

The Hartland Model

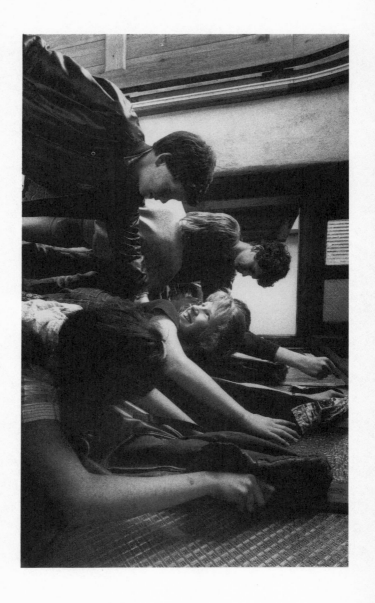

The Hartland
Model

I ARRIVED at Hartland Small School on a bright
summer Wednesday. This is the afternoon the children go in for sports and exercise. Indeed, there had been
some discussion from the authorities about the idea of a
secondary school without facilities suitable to the modern
pursuit of the body beautiful. No gym? Where are the
parallel bars and the football pitch?

I arrived too late for the lunch that one of the teachers
and two or three of the children had prepared for the rest of
the school. Luckily, they had saved some; delicious
spaghetti and sauce (vegetarian), and brown rolls, and rich
Devon butter on them.

Some of the children were off to play tennis on the
village courts. The rest of us piled into two cars and headed
down to Hartland Quay. It is a place of surpassing natural
beauty. A. E. Trueman's *Geology and Scenery in England
and Wales (Penguin, 1972)*, the Bible of such matters, gives
the area several pages, and Hartland emerges as one of its
jewels. Its shales and sandstones are turned through ninety
degrees, into the vertical; but they have been bent and
contorted into wonderful swirls. This is, says Trueman, a
"bleak and rugged coast, characteristically dark grey or
brown in colour. The cliffs are never dull, however, they

have such diversity of form, their dark colours react to every change in sky or sunlight, and vegetation brightens every ledge."

On this summer's day there was pretty little evidence of the dark and bleak side to things. The ocean was clear, greeny-blue and inviting. Under the eye of two teachers, the youngsters struck out across the bay from the stone pier, in a gentle swim to a cove of shingle where they swam and played until they were tired and then they lay down amongst the rocks.

Six older ones — three boys and three girls — struck out more adventurously. Strung out in line abreast, they headed off out to sea, to where a steep off-shore island jutted out of the waves. It took them maybe ten minutes of strong, confident swimming to get there. They fooled around amongst the rocks on the water's edge for a while and then the girls turned back for home. I saw three boys clamber up the steep island side: high up, until they found a comfortable grassy perch on which to loll. There they soaked up the sun and, I imagine, gossiped awhile.

When it was time to go back to school, we waved towels at them and they turned back.

It would be fatal to make a piece of sociology out of this small episode. But it was the kind of thing any one of us might hope some children, somewhere, were having the fun of. It was the stuff childhood memories are made of: casual, friendly, athletic, challenging, easeful.

In the context of a 'school' day it was remarkable, of course.

First, the teachers knew the degree to which they could trust the children. They watched what was going on, but had little need to influence it. They knew what the children and the children's parents would allow and accept. Secondly, the children knew that they were up to the swim and were free to act on their confident knowledge. Thirdly, there was a richly physical activity (several: swimming, climbing, soaking up the sun). Fourthly, there was challenge but not competition (nothing wrong with competition, of course; but challenge is pretty good too). Fifthly, there was an aesthetic element: a conventional sports ground is a grassy desert; mown and manicured grass from which all floristic interest has been systematically, and expensively, banished; but this sea was lovely. Sixthly, the children were indulged and allowed in an activity very precious to them: time to chat and define their own activities.

I heard no cross words; no shouting; no anger. Just everything any adult hopes children can be: co-operative, strong, happy, orderly, adventurous.

There were other children on that pier that day. Two were being looked after by a woman I took to be their mother. Big lads, dithering at the edge of the pier, wondering whether to take the plunge and dive into the briny. She said they should. We all said they should. They dithered and havered for a while longer. Finally, shrieking with delight, they were in, and loving it.

The woman told me that they were two boys from a local comprehensive: a big school, of the kind you often found in country districts, to which children are bussed from miles around. She was a special teacher who devoted her time to the disruptive children and tried to get them to enjoy themselves and school a bit more. Coming to Hartland was, she says, a special treat for them. A good couple of days' application, and they could come to the Quay for a bathe. "Look at them," she said, affectionately. "They don't look as though they could be the terror of the school, do they? All they need is attention."

And so it was that the children from the Small School — whose sports afternoon was likely to be an impoverished affair because they had to swim in the open sea — were doing so for fun and as a matter of normality what in the local comprehensive — with all its gyms and equipment —

was regarded as a therapeutic treat for the delinquent. Odd, perhaps, that the boys from the comprehensive had to be naughty to 'earn' the special treatment of a Hartland swim. Odder still that their school is precisely the establishment from which several children have been withdrawn in order that they should go to Hartland.

The Small School at Hartland was started in 1982. Satish Kumar, the editor of *Resurgence* (the magazine of the 'alternative' world both spiritual and practical) and chairman of the Schumacher Society, and his wife June had been living in the village for some years. Their daughter and son Mukti were at the local primary school. But Mukti, then aged 9, was faced with the prospect of going to Bideford Comprehensive School. Satish and June did not feel that a school with nearly 2000 on the roll was the right place for a family with convictions of a 'small is beautiful' kind. Satish did not relish his son commuting to a school fifteen miles away. And Bideford School did not have the kind of reputation which encouraged him.

Satish decided that he should set about starting a school along the lines which he preferred. It would be small. It would be a day school only, and depend on people who could reach it on a daily basis. It especially ought to draw support from the whole community. It would encourage children to learn how to learn rather than teach them a strictly defined curriculum. The children would cook their school lunch and clean up the premises after their day's work. The children would be consulted on policy.

There was, by chance, a Methodist chapel in the village: it came up for sale as these thoughts were maturing. Drawing on the extensive *Resurgence* network, Satish was able to go to the the auction confident that £20,000 could be found to buy the buildings. It turned out that this was the figure which secured the property for the Small School: it was also the figure that a local builder was very near to being prepared to pay for the building (so the *Resurgence* readers' investment in the bricks and mortar was safe; shares have since changed hands).

Satish Kumar was soon in touch with the County Education Office, and its Director, who was less than enthusiastic that the Small School project was something his authority could support in any way. "We had," says Satish, "quite a heated argument." He learned that day that Devon Education Authority was paying £6 million a year bussing children to its schools: it has become a war cry with Satish that he could do great things with that 6 million.

Satish Kumar is keen that his small school should one day attract some sort of state support. To this end he has invited Exeter University's School of Education to monitor the educational progress of the school. He also has tacit agreement from Devon's L.E.A. that they will look at the evidence as it becomes available.

Meanwhile, the Small School is receiving grant aid from various charities, and perhaps most significantly from the Sainsbury Trust which particularly stipulated that its interest depended on there being a principle — some value as a model — behind the Small School: the trust was concerned to discover some generalisations about small schools.

Whilst the children swam that afternoon, I sat on the pier with Colin Hodgetts, the Church of England clergyman who is headmaster of the Small School. He is the author of a book on worship, meditation and yoga, and of a modern-style hymnal, full of good songs for schools and gatherings. He has worked with refugees and in charities concerned with the poor world. He has taught in a church school in

London's inner city. He and his wife have been doing up the derelict barn they bought near Hartland, so as to be near Colin's new job. He took up his £5,500 a year appointment in 1983.

I asked him whether it was wise to dispense with a formal curriculum in which subjects are defined and divided into compartments under specialist teachers. "I think it's very odd the way that though we learn like magpies, we try to teach systematically, as though information was divided up like that in the world. Besides, it's very important when you look at the curricular claims of a school to find out what is really on offer. Often it looks much grander than it actually is in practice."

Elsewhere, he has written that he dislikes examinations altogether as a system of judging children, and would encourage even an exam-minded family to restrict their child's 'O' Levels to perhaps five subjects, holding the view that even that number would unduly restrict the 'real' education of the child. Few professions need more than that number of 'O' Levels. Beyond that, an academic child would probably do better to go on to a sixth form college for 'A' Levels, and thence to university. A two-and-a-half teacher secondary school inevitably would have some difficulty satisfying the very academic child after 'O' Level.

But up to that level of attainment, Colin Hodgetts is confident. "I am sure we couldn't do much to prevent a child getting on at 'O' Level!" Behind the blyth comment there is a certain awareness that by encouraging curiosity and learning, the Small School may paradoxically be doing more for its academic children than the comprehensive in which a bright child may be putting up with a good deal of difficulty from the environment around him.

"I am thoroughly convinced that a child comes to school to work. I've been reading a book about some Italian peasant children who ran their own school, and taught one another. The children wrote of those from another village who visited them: 'they had never heard that one goes to school to learn, and that to go is a privilege.'

That evening a group of children went up to Colin's house for a discussion about a music week which the school was going to embark on. First, one of the girls cast an eye over Colin's crop of grass, which might be useful for her pony. Someone made tea. We toured the building work: painstakingly, some rather good and imaginative joinery work is turning the barn into what will be a very chic home. The mother cat had been killing mice to show her kittens the way of it: a couple of headless corpses had to be disposed of.

Then we gathered for a discussion. Would this piano teacher turn up? Could an amplifier be wrung from an elder brother? Could the school divide into groups for the composing of songs? What about a cappella, a la The Flying Pickets — could the sheet music be found? There were recollections of the day a steel band had come. And of some Ghanaian drummers. Of a bad day when the school had notably not responded to an invited drama teacher's imaginative schemes: it had been a Friday, and one should not aim for much energy late on a Friday. Indeed, the afternoons of a summer's day tend to be a little restive altogether.

The children were developing a healthy appetite for the composing of a programme. "What if some of them don't like what we suggest?" asked one girl. "Well," said a boy, "We could always just say to them, right, if you know so much, why don't you come up with a better programme?"

We ended up with a list of activities which ought to be incorporated in the week: Making Instruments; Playing Music Together; Playing in Groups; Imitating Singers; Improvising; Dancing to Recorded Music; Dancing to Our Own Music; Teaching Each Other How to Read Music;

Exploring Rhythm. "When we plan these things," said Mukti, "we always find there isn't time to develop any one of them properly."

And then some of the group went home, whilst others joined a party to drive into Barnstaple for a London touring production of *Waiting for Godot*.

The next day, Mukti walked with me from his house up to the school. Nine o'clock, and the old Methodist chapel is beginning to be busy. There are 27 pupils at the school. Most of them are in school today.

The main room of the chapel is shaped pretty much as any school hall in Victoria's time must have been. But there are no desks, only tables scattered about. This is where the school takes lunch: in 'family' (cross-aged) groups, with an adult at each table. There is a vast book case, made by one of the parents and full of books. A weaver's loom stands ready by the door. The children have locker space, unlocked. There is a little more clutter than would have suited the stricter sort of 'school-marm'.

At the back of the room, there is the kitchen. This week is one of a series towards the end of each term in which the school devotes itself to a particular subject: at the moment it is food, and in honour of the occasion the headmaster is to cook an exotic dessert.

Up some stairs, there is another room, large and carpeted, in which chairs have been placed in a circle. As school is convened we all sit in the round. Colin Hodgetts picks up his guitar and, one hand riffling through his beard, picks a song from his own collection. He sets us off with a chord or two and his own strong voice. The children join in, but not with notable enthusiasm, I note with relief: I don't think children who took schooling with *too* much enthusiasm would be quite normal.

One of the parents who comes in to teach and help has brought with her a book of William Cobbett's and launches into his account of how much superior the brewing of beer is over the brewing of tea. The children do their best to sit quietly and attentively, but minds wander.

Then there is a minute or two's silence. It reminds me of the periods of silence we used to have at my prep school: in that case we would lie in the school hall after lunch, and be played classical music on a scratchy pre-hi-fi. The Hartland silence seems rather a sound moment of recollection in busy lives.

After this assembly, people scattered. Most of the pupils were engaged in writing up the results of projects undertaken earlier in the week. One fellow of perhaps twelve, a skinny local boy who struck me as a bit nervous and lacking in confidence, was trying to settle down to write about the history of the chocolate business in England. He was friendly but shy and making little progress. He had been taken away from the local comprehensive by his parents. He was doing better now than he had there. He was happier. Doubtless, he was going to develop fast.

A big farming family son, Billy Jewell, made it clear to me that he was a bit sceptical about the 'fringe' element about the school: nothing overt, but plenty of flourishing of big tractor brochures and sturdy defence of 'proper' farming and eating habits over anything too organic and vegetarian. But he too had been an unhappy pupil at the big Bideford Comprehensive. Paradoxically, he was so big at twelve and thirteen that the sixteen year-olds had taken to giving him a hard time. He was a very tall boy, clearly dedicated to his farm, and a snappy dresser.

I came across other people here and there: one girl (I later found she had written a lovely account of her first days at school) was reading at a bench in the garden. She could not speak, having taken a sponsored vow of silence for the day (she was tricked out of it at lunch by mistake: found

herself saying 'thank you'.) One or two were working in the
diminutive science lab with Maggie Agg, the school's
science specialist, whose own children are scattered between
the village primary (thriving) and the Small School. There
was a glass tank in the lab, full of micro-pondlife and the
vigorous carnivores within it.

In the kitchen, two of the children were doing lunch:
chopping salad things, lots of them, this being a salad-fest.
The smell of baking filled the rooms. In the caretaker's
kitchen next door, some more children were making jam. In
the hall, vast flagons of wine were fermenting: the result,
partly scientific, partly bucolic, partly bacchanalian, of a
previous day's work.

Half way through the morning, the art teacher arrived.
She was in stripey dungarees, and seemed distinctly sparky:
vivid and lively. Mukti was soon at work on a bizarre,
modernist creation involving vivid geometric patterns,
Germanic-looking insignia, starbursts and so on: it would
have made a record sleeve for a hard rock band. But it had
about it neatness and precision as well as imagination. One
of Billy's drawings was pointed out to me: delicate, careful,
accurate. Now he was developing a tractorish theme. Others
were sketching from nature outside.

We began lunch with the Peace Prayer, the saying of
which marks out any gathering as being authentically
'alternative'. I have yet to overcome my resistance to its
goofy modernness, but have to accept that it is quite
handsome. And then we went up by tables to serve
ourselves from the six or seven salad bowls arrayed at a
buffet table. Colin Hodgetts was busy in the kitchen,
preparing his pudding. When a woman from a radio station
came in to interview him, he swept down the hall toward
her, saying, "I'm afraid you'll have to wait just a little while.
I'm preparing Baked Alaska for the school."

It was delicious, and a useful lesson for a school whose
afternoon was to be spent discussing some of the extrava-

gances of the Western diet. There were several possible lessons to be derived from the dish: for instance, about the insulating properties of bought sponge and meringue, as they both cooked without melting the ice cream within. "Of course," said the chef, "you can't cook a Baked Alaska in a microwave oven." But the best lesson was that no one can live the pure, wholesome, worthy, wholefood life all the time. Man does not live by whole wheat bread alone.

Colin went to speak to the radio lady's tape recorder. "I became involved in this school in its second year because I was aware that there were a lot of problems with state schools. But I am not interested in it as a model for small private schools, but to show that it is possible for small schools to work, and that the state could do it. We want to provide — we do provide — a school for children of all backgrounds. We don't have an 'alternative' set of values. We work with children's homes, not against them. We have parents here with *'Guardian'* values; and we also have children from families with very traditional farming values. We have dairy farmers and vegetarians. We have to keep all these balls in the air. That is what it means to have a community school.

"We try to achieve this by three main means. We visit all the homes and sit down with the child and his or her parents to discuss their schooling. We have three meetings a term with all the parents and those kids that want to come. And we keep in touch with the home."

He was asked what sanctions the school used in cases of ill-discipline.

"The other children would speak to anyone who was disrupting their time here. And we would talk to the parents as well. I suppose, in the end, we would have to send the child home. I've only had to do it twice in my couple of years here. Fundamentally, we aim to turn the whole thing on its head. At most schools, if you're badly behaved, you're kept in. But if you keep people in, you turn the place into a prison. We prefer to get children into the point of view where they see it as a privilege to come to school."

What about the difficulty that a school with so few children did not provide each child with a sufficient range of friends? Not a big enough peer-group? Colin was almost impatient in his reply. "But surely all through people's lives they have to learn to make friends amongst a rather small, and given, group? It happens in the family, it happens in the workplace. Getting on with a given group, and learning to co-operate with them, is surely very important."

He had already talked to me a little about his feeling that a family atmosphere at school is important. "Youngsters need a protective environment whilst they are going through adolescence: they've enough going on internally without a lot of extra pressures. But once they're through that period, and are beginning to have the confidence of an adult, that's the time to go out and face the world's difficulties. That's why we don't trouble the children here with an enormously complicated view of the wider world; there's time enough for that, and all the difficulties that go with it. Mind you, even if we were inclined to be, let's say, in favour of C.N.D. or something like that we would have a tremendous job fighting the scepticism of the children themselves. It really does make me laugh when people say that children are being brainwashed by things like 'peace studies': have you ever tried to persuade a child of something he doesn't believe?"

I wanted to talk to some parents, especially those 'native' Devon people from the village and around. The first was the mother of the shy boy who had been working on the project on chocolate. She runs a shop in the village: on the surface an ordinary small-village business, but with clear signs of imagination and skill at work in it. The books on the shelves in the back room were middle- to high-brow. The mother was frankly concerned that at the Small School her son was not getting a traditional education. But she accepted that he had been very unhappy at the comprehensive in Bideford.

"I don't think they care about exams at all at the Small School. It's true that they don't matter in themselves, but they are useful. I worked in a bank without any exams myself, but they wouldn't let you do that today. And it's all very well for Colin not to worry about them — he wouldn't be where he is without them, would he? But my son loves that school, and that's something, isn't it?"

On balance, she thought she had made the right decision in making the change.

I got myself asked to lunch at the Jewell farm, a few miles out of Hartland. Anne was cooking beef and masses of vegetables, and whilst we waited for her husband and a friend of his (they were sheep shearing) to turn up, she told me a bit about her family. Her husband John was born on the farm, whilst she was born in Hartland itself. Her two daughters did well at school; now one works for the International Labour Organisation in Geneva, and the other is married to a Guatemalan electrical engineer ("For him Sir Francis Drake is no hero, just a maritime robber") and lives in Cologne. She misses them both, but enjoys the diversity they have found.

It's a farm of 170 acres, with pedigree limousin cattle, a dairy herd and sheep. Anne and John strike one as robust and loving people; not notably progressive in their views on morality probably (but what family-minded person is?), and perfectly well aware that farming is a changing business. They and the Kumars like each other a good deal: "There's nothing hippy about Satish," said Anne, even as she expressed her doubts about the Small School.

They are considerable, though friendly. With young Billy coming home with bruises from the comprehensive, it was clear something had to be done. "We could probably have sorted that out in the end. But he didn't seem to be learning anything either. I mean he came home one day and asked if Devon was in England. That wouldn't do.

"I'll be frank with you. If I could've afforded the local public school, I'd have sent him there as a day boy. The girls went to the convent at Bideford, and it was absolutely wonderful. That's what I would have liked for Billy. I wouldn't like to send him away, though.

"Anyway, the Small School came up, and a couple of his friends were going there, and so he thought it might be better. He's certainly happy there. But that's not everything.

"He has made some very beautiful things in wood: that carved owl, that lampstand and a recorder." They are all workmanlike efforts, and the owl is really lovely. "But I'm not sure he knows how to make a sentence, or the difference between a paragraph and a sentence.

"But I do see that he's just not the kind to come home and take down a book. His father's a wonderful man, but he never reads a book. Neither Billy nor John is the kind of person to get lost in a book. We watch things like *Horizon* on television, so we know a lot of what's going on.

"Billy just wants to get on to the farm when he comes home from school. He wants to look after the stock or get on a tractor. But he realises that farming is changing and that he'll have to be a different kind of farmer than his father or grandfather were. We're looking at getting a computer, and Billy's already started doing some typing at the Small School, so as to be better on the keyboard when we do."

Anne Jewell is clearly the kind of woman on whom any community venture depends: she is talented, sensible, and open-minded. I asked her why, if she had worries about the school, she did not get down there and see for herself, at length and in detail, what was going on? If she had a worry about Billy's sentences and spelling, why not go into the school and help him with them?

"I know I ought to," she said. "But I'd feel awkward in the Small School."

This is crucial surely? The traditional, conservative, meat-eating, 'straight' world feels excluded from the free-thinking, vegetarian, articulate world. But the Small School needs Anne Jewell, even more than Anne Jewell needs it.

There is no dispute about this. Everyone connected with the Small School knows that it will survive, and be worth having, only if it becomes a proper expression of the world around it, in which craftsmen (of the old and new waves), farmers (of the old and new waves) and anyone else lucky enough to live in so lovely a spot, all contrive to bring an influence to bear on it.

The Small School is committed to community education. This implies a two-way relationship between a school and the people around it. First, the school hopes that adult people will come to it, either to learn or to teach; and second, that children from the school will go into the community.

The Hartland school will be preserved from becoming a ghetto-school — a school for vegetarians, or a school for bucolics — because it must serve the wider, extremely modern community of Hartland in which many different sorts of people live. The idea of 'community' is and always has been complicated. The word is hardly ever used without people being aware of an irony: that wherever you have a strong community there is almost always a concomitant tension and internecine division. Worse, in a way, wherever there is an emphasis on 'community', people run the risk of claustrophobic parochialism. There is nothing like a strong community for breeding in its young a desire to break out and see the world.

But even allowing for the way that 'community' is a buzz-word, covers a multitude of sins, and connotes ideas which are often pretty phoney, it is also a useful code word for the idea that a neighbourhood needs to know and sustain itself in order to provide a decent environment in which to live.

In the case of the Small School, one boy — who has now left — became a competent roofer by going out with a roofer for a spell and learning the trade. Other children have repaired a broken-down tractor *in situ* with a skilled mechanic. Children learn pottery in the studio of a famous potter. They learn the management of a dairy by going to a farm, and cheese-making by spending hours with professional cheese-makers.

One morning, I drove down to Gloucestershire to join up with Satish whilst he was walking round the country on a pilgrimage, undertaken in something of a Hindu spirit. He had just turned fifty; took no money; depended on the small but vigorous and nationwide circle of *Resurgence* readers for accommodation, food, directions.

The sun was warm, and he set a cracking pace. "The oddest thing about education is that we have completely forgotten to teach children by getting them to *do*. Think of the way we teach the English language: people spend hours learning how Shakespeare wrote plays, but not how to write plays. We learn how other people did things, not how to do them ourselves. But Shakespeare did not go to university to learn how to write plays; he learned by doing.

"The children at the Small School, according to some people, do not have the right sort of opportunities; people say we could not supply sufficient facilities. But the children learn pottery from Philip Leach, grandson of Bernard Leach. The writer, John Moat, comes in to help them with a writing week. A doctor used to come in and teach biology — that was before Maggie Agg joined us. We take children to a basket-maker so that they can learn basket-making. Four or five children at a time learn cheese-making with another person.

"Part of why this is so good is that the children learn

these things from people who are making a living at it. They learn the attitude and atmosphere needed to make a skill pay. We keep reading that children are not learning how to be commercial and self-reliant in schools. But here in the little Hartland School — so short of facilities apparently! — the children are learning to be self-reliant. Our children will go out into the world not needing to have someone else to provide a job for them, but be able and willing to make a job for themselves."

It would be a very limited education (though thorough, and richer than many) which allowed Hartland children a close view only of the local world, however bustling and beautiful. So the Small School prides itself on attracting a wide range of people to visit it and speak. Steel bands, dancers, African drummers have all visited. Sir George Trevelyan, John Seymour and many others have spoken. The children are also used to having people from radio, the press and television around: a mixed blessing, perhaps; but at least to be dealing with media people goes towards developing all those 'communication' skills which are prized these days. The children at Hartland Small School know how to deal with strangers; they know how to look them in the eye and talk to them and answer questions about themselves. How many employers have sighed for those simple skills in the youngsters they interview?

On the second day of my Hartland visit, a group of fifth and sixth formers from India, together with their hosts from Milton Keynes, were due to visit the Small School, during their stay in Devon. The Indian children were due to cook lunch for the Devonians.

Hartland is not the kind of small English village which is fazed by the sudden call for garlic, chilli and cardamom: the grocer's store readily produced all these and more. One or two children affected not to like curry, but most were well used to it. The school was, of course, perfectly used to the business of cooking being part of the day. Indeed, no school could be as well adjusted to the idea of a group of people preparing food and then enjoying it as part of the educative day.

After lunch, Indian dancing, with many of the Hartland children learning how to join in. And then a return match: the Hartland children had prepared a cream tea for their overseas visitors.

Then one or two of the Indians described their school day. It sounded very traditonal: modelled on the routine of an English public school. It sounded, indeed, as though in India the kind of regimented, disciplined, subject-oriented, curriculum-bound school which we are finding our way out of was the prized privilege of the lucky few who can be sent from their villages, towns and cities to experience it. I suggested to one of the accompanying Indian teachers that many of us were envious of the tradition which we have largely lost and which India still preserves. She would have none of it: what use was it, she said, for a country to devote its best educational resources to giving an old-fashioned academic education to children who needed a practical one?

She would have been the kind of person exactly to support the spirit of education being fostered at Hartland.

I was still nagged by an anxiety that a bright, highly-motivated child could succeed at Hartland; a practical, non-academic child might flourish there; a spiritual child might perform extraordinarily; but what about the lazy bright child, or the child whose mind is slow, but quite efficient? What about, in other words, the kinds of children for whom structure, method, organisation, might be a rather good way of learning?

On my last day, I looked through some essays by three or four children. Two of the offerings I could perhaps have predicted: they came from the kind of children of whom fluency and creativity of a high order might be expected. What I did not expect was the dedication to neatness and structure: in the midst of creative ferment there was evidence of discipline, too. In another of the offerings there was maturity beyond the years of the child who had done the writing: perhaps the maturity of tone which a self-consciously literate child might have — but what a luxury to have it. But one boy, of whom I would have expected much less, did a very creditable piece of writing too. He was a boy who had — I suspect — been through a pretty rough time at previous schools: he was clearly making progress fast.

CHAPTER FOUR

The Lewknor
Model

The Lewknor
Model

NEAR OXFORD there is a small local authority village
school which bears all the signs of being a traditional
primary establishment. It was a hundred and fifty years old
last year (1986). It has a thatched roof. It has a population
which varies, according to the year, between forty and fifty
pupils. It is thus regarded officially as being well below the
sort of size which should be technically feasible.

For the past fifteen years, up till his departure last
summer, it has had a very remarkable headmaster, Mervyn
Benford. Mr Benford is probably the greatest exponent of
the art of running the small school in the Western world. He
has travelled from New Zealand to Sweden seeing schools,
and learning about the problems and advantages they have.

He is a fierce proponent of the good sense of educating
children near their homes, and in the sort of schools where
they can know their place and feel comfortable in it.

Yet his two most important ideas have nothing to do
with the size of the school, particularly. They could both be
instituted at any time in a school whose nominal population
was 50, 500 or 5000.

The first is that the world's knowledge is not divided
into curriculum subjects, such as geography, history or

English. So, he feels, teaching should reflect this by breaking down the artificial barriers between the bits of our understanding of the world. He is firm that one would see all these different subjects flowing through the course of a child's day at Lewknor; but there would be less formal labelling.

We will see how the curriculum-driven school has an inbuilt engine for largeness. But this new breaking down of the curricula has another merit. This is that a child should begin not to notice the distinction between practice and theory, and between science and art. Practice and science should be felt as flowing from theory and art (or *vice versa*).

In proposing ideas such as this, Mr Benford is challenging the entire edifice of education, and he therefore does so with as much modesty as a very determined man may. Certainly, he finds that the children of Lewknor are not turned out so revolutionary that they find the transition to the local secondary school too difficult.

The other idea runs counter to one of the most strongly-held and absurdly counter-productive shibboleths of the school system. This is that each school must be divided into classes, and these must reflect either the child's age, or the child's attainment. There is hot dispute within the school system as to which is the better of these two methods of deciding whether a child 'goes up' or 'stays down' in a particular class at the end of the year.

Once in his or her group, the child normally stays in it to learn, to play, to read, to paint, to do maths.

At Lewknor, with beautiful simplicity, this is all thrown over. At this school, a child joins a sort of family group of children, whose ages will spread from top to bottom of the age range in the place, and will have a class teacher whose role is to watch over that group as custodian of the well-being of each individual in it, both academic and social.

Some of the teaching is done by age, some by ability,

and some in the very mixed 'family' group. But the point is that the child does not have an identity by virtue of some narrow definition of similarity (of age or attainment or ability) but by being part of some much wider and more interesting group.

Flowing from this idea and practice, at Lewknor one finds one child helping another, and learning both more about what he or she knows (by having to communicate it) and about the world of co-operation.

Now, many people would intuitively feel, or could come to realise, that this is an agreeable way of teaching children; that they learn a lot about the world in such wide groups; that the models of behaviour they would pick up from this system would be supportive and encouraging and would reflect the width of relationships one has in the real world.

This absence of 'streaming', this abolition of the 'peer' group, is, however, regarded as one of the most sharp reasons why small schools cannot work.

In other words, a small school is forced into mixing children up (because it does not have a big enough population to make sufficiently large groups of equal age or attainment). But this mixing things up in small schools is not a reason to abolish them; rather one should see it as a model for mixing up other schools more.

There is a far stronger prejudice in educational circles against 'mixed' classes than any of the scant available evidence could allow. In various papers, a team headed by Professor Neville Bennett (then of Lancaster University, and now of Exeter) have suggested that even in present mixed classes, which have come about because of falling rolls and some tightening of budgets, there is precious little evidence that any harm flows from it.

This work suggests that in many schools, teachers do see the social — the human — and even the educational advantages of mixing up classes: that it seems not to hold up the brighter children and does avoid stigmatising the less able. But it is a demanding system of schooling children, and may even be more prone to being done badly than the present streaming by age or otherwise.

But it is important to note that mixed classes have only been researched because they are perceived as a problem: introduced unwillingly by schools which had no experience or commitment to the system, mixed classes were then looked at in an exercise to see how much damage had been done.

Typically of educational research, the results do not tell you that mixed classes are better than single age or attainment classes. They only tell you that, done well, either seems to work; done badly, neither does. We are free to begin with the practice which suits our other requirements or matches our intuitions.

Lewknor School has interesting things to say about some other problems associated with small schools. One is to do with its only attracting from the education authority a salary for two-and-a-bit teachers. The answer is to do some very effective fund-raising. Lewknor is not a rich village, but it raises £1000 a year towards a salary for a third teacher, and the school goes to foundations for further funding.

This is likely to be a major hang-up with many people: surely a state system should provide the teachers and the books needed to give children an education? Surely to breach this principle is to risk throwing all its virtues away? Surely poor neighbourhoods will not be able to match the commitment that a rich neighbourhood can?

But actually, the more a school is dependent on its community for help, the more both the school and the community can express themselves by their mutual inter-dependence. And though the rich neighbourhood can find money easily, there is a strong and under-used argument that a poor community has large numbers of unemployed people, and these could be brought into greater contact with the school in their midst either for manual or teaching work or both.

I once attended a meeting at a small fishing town in the North-East which had 60 per cent unemployment amongst its adults. But the town's population of children had fallen below some magic number and the authority had told the town that their school could have an educational budget which paid for two and half teachers. The school needed three teachers, the authority decreed. So the local school should close. The children could walk or be bussed to the next town. The town was incensed. But it occurred to no-one that the town should have demanded the retention of the school, and of two teachers paid for by the authority, with the other half salary going to library or other services, and the teaching shortfall made up with volunteer effort from 160 adults there who had, tragically, no work.

This sort of idea is anathema to pure socialism or even to impure socialism. But it is practical for all that.

Perhaps there is a let-out here. Perhaps the state should indeed wholly fund only schools of the kind it approves. But as parents and others set up or propose different models, then the community at large should feel free to invest time, energy and money in these alternatives.

There is a feeling around in socialist thinking that independent fee-paying schools are in themselves a bad thing because they give the rich an advantage which they can buy. The independent school movement I and many others now propose would in effect be giving the children from any background the means of giving and receiving the commitment and motivation which is far more valuable than anything money can buy.

Education is not, after all, something one consumes, or something which is delivered. It is not a thing but a process. It will be excellent or appalling, in some important degree, in proportion to the effort which goes into it on the part of all concerned. State 'provision' of education is already in danger of being just that: something which is meted out, and placed in front of pupils for them to pick up or leave alone at whim. That is in some sense inevitable to state provision of anything, and is not an argument for abolishing it if there is nothing to take its place. But that the state provides a service is no reason at all to frown on the idea of other competitive models springing up.

One of the most important ideas which is taking hold now is that children do not actually need to spend their school lives in the company only of teachers and other pupils. Indeed, since they can learn very little about nursing, car mechanics, running a small shop, or a big one, or being a poet, say, from most teachers, there is every reason to suppose that many of the things they need to know they cannot learn in school.

There is an emerging idea that teachers should not always, or as a matter of first preference, teach the children directly. Instead, they should become brokers between the children and the army of adults with whom they need educative contact. The teachers can help the amateur and volunteer and part-time 'teachers' to do well in the unfamiliar classroom, and the teacher can consolidate later what the child has learned or been inspired to discover from a visitor from outside.

At Lewknor, they are very keen on the outside world coming into the school, and also go to great lengths to take the children to museums.

This is an idea which is very attractive to small schools because it overcomes the inherent narrowness of the range that one or two teachers can bring to the classroom, and it helps to overcome the sense of isolation that must come to many small school teachers. But it is not one that should be confined to small schools, though it may most powerfully grow there. All children deserve to meet a wide range of adults: it should not merely be a privilege for those that go to small schools.

Another method of overcoming the difficulties of small schools may have relevance well beyond them. In the mid-seventies, as various education authorities considered what to do with their scattered small schools, there was much discussion of what could be achieved by schools forming loose federations amongst themselves. In this way they could share a peripatetic teacher, for instance, or even shunt children around amongst themselves.

These considerations are very important in view of the cost argument which is often used against small schools. Local authorities are inclined to point out that in some counties the cost of teaching a child in a small school may be nearly twice that of teaching him or her in a large school. The logical thought, then, is to close the small school.

However, Mervyn Benford, in a study he made during a sabbatical from teaching, found that there was a wide range in amounts spent by small schools on each pupil, just as there was in big schools. But no-one proposed, he noted, the closure of large schools which looked budgetarily inefficient.

Sometimes, if there is a nearby school with spare 'capacity' going begging, the local authority can make an enormous saving by closing small schools.

However, the main fixed cost in teaching children is in providing the teacher. He or she makes up between 60 and 70 per cent of the cost of educating the child. Clearly, the volunteer could make a substantial difference to the funding of education and the viability of all sorts of different educational institutions, including small schools.

Even so, because the educational prejudice currently reinforces the bureaucratic urge towards neatness in encouraging authorities to close small schools, it seems to be the case that authorities are not over-scrupulous about looking at the cost-benefits of closing small schools, case by case. The displaced children may need building work to be done on their new school; there will probably be bussing expenses. Indeed, the latest and most thorough look at small schools and their closure suggests that most school closure involved, taking transport and other things into consideration, the saving of one teacher's salary.

It may be that small schools and their parents will have to accept that the system they approve of requires a community subsidy equivalent to one teacher's pay over and above what the state allows.

Yet even here, there are moves which suggest that the overview of the local authority, and their budgetary control, may not be the most efficient. In one scheme, in Cambridgeshire, schools were encouraged to take command of their own budgets, and allocate spending as they chose.

Most of the savings in the Cambridgeshire scheme were marginal, but one school was able to employ two extra teachers and several have bought new books.

This is just another example of the way in which new practices can go toward diversity, autonomy and excellence.

At Lewknor, we have a school which is, beside the church and the pub, one of the landmarks of the place. It is also the seat of an educational 'regime' which some would call an 'experiment'. But it has been going on for fifteen years, evolving all the time, and is now going to be carried on by a new headmistress who believes in the basic guidelines which have been laid down.

It is a school which has attracted a small amount of dissent within the locality, perhaps because some parents fear that it is extraordinarily novel and therefore risky.

I read some very good writing when I was there, and also sat next to a child who clearly had great difficulty with her work. At a singing rehearsal, I saw the normal signs of a bored child or two, and experienced just as much evidence of wonderfully interested and engaged children.

Most parents, visiting the school, spending any time they could spare around the place, would, I think, say they had found one of those happy schools we all dream of for our children. One mother came up to me and said the school had transformed her children, and would by itself have merited moving out of London.

CHAPTER FIVE

The Danish Model

The Danish Model

DENMARK IS an extraordinary country for an English-man to visit. It is so easeful to one's eye and ear. People there are quiet, almost quaint. But they are also efficient and liberated. They seem to be a people without litter or hang-ups. They are old-fashioned and modern at once. They smoke and drink and sail boats, and they don't seem to argue too much amongst themselves.

They also have small schools as a matter of course. These flourishing institutions seem to have grown out of some of the national characteristics I've described. They have grown out of a national awareness of casual tolerance; of the encouragement of diversity; of national consensus; of a delight in excellence and a relaxed commitment to the good life.

In Denmark, something over 8 per cent of the country's children — and over 20 per cent of children from Copenhagen, the capital city — attend private schools in which the parents, pupils and teachers are bound (as to some extent they are in any Danish school) to come together to thrash out any policy. About 14 per cent of Danish schools are in the independent, state-subsidised sector.

But the ethos of these schools is not snobbish, though

in some it may be elitist, or at least (and how odd that such a thing might be said pejoratively) oriented towards excellence of academic achievement.

The independent school movement in Denmark does not depend on the affluence of individual parents. It is of course a country with a much higher per capita income than our own: but to send a child to a Danish independent school costs a parent something like £30 a month. Normally, the second child sent from a family attracts a big discount, and so on, until the fourth would go quite free. The state funds these schools to the tune of about 85 per cent of their expenditure.

The independent small schools of Denmark cost more per pupil to run overall, but cost the state rather less, than the equivalent public or state schools. In practice, the parents and others meet between 20 and 25 per cent of the costs, not the 15 per cent notionally expected. The state pays for the transportation of children living a certain distance away from the school.

Accounts differ radically of the constraints the schools work under. I have heard it said that Denmark can afford, culturally, to have these independent, but state-funded, private schools because it imposes a curriculum upon them. In other words, the argument goes, centrally-directed sets of standards dictate that the school's independence is thoroughly limited. But two headmasters of such places told me that they had complete freedom to teach what they liked, provided only that arithmetic and Danish figured in the syllabus. Each school must appoint, subject to Ministry of Education approval, an overseer, responsible to the Ministry for ensuring that the private school matches the performance of state schools.

In practice, they said, there was little difficulty because the parents, teachers and pupils would hardly bother to work within or with a school that did not 'deliver' a well-educated child, fit for Danish social and economic life.

"We are the salt in the wounds of the state education service," said the headmaster of one such school. The spectre of competition kept the state system up to the mark. His school had been started in one of the most northerly towns in Denmark over one hundred years ago, as a school to provide country girls of the better-off farmers with an education fitted to their station in life. In other words, it was advanced in its desire to see girls succeed, but wholly pragmatic in its acceptance that private enterprise would be needed to pay for the fulfilment of the aspiration.

Now the school is housed in a suburb of the town. It is brand, spanking new. There are 342 children in the school, with a thriving pre-school centre. The six-year-olds do not do a full day, but are looked after all day if working parents need the service. The school caters for children until they leave for university.

The headmaster was frank. "I think I should say that we have a sort of rule here. The most important thing for us is not the creative thing; it is the book. We have to work a little harder here, I think: the children must learn more here, or else the parents would not pay for them to come. It is the same with disruptive children: parents do not pay for their children to come to a school where there is a lot of noise in class. And if a child is very naughty we can say, 'if you do not like it here, we shall have to let you go back to the public school.' That is an advantage, because few children would like to go back. But of course the state schools do not have that sort of advantage!"

This sort of view might convey an impression of easy elitism and of narrow competitiveness in the ethos of such a school. But behind the specially-designed ergonomic school desks and chairs, it was obvious that the school was a place bursting with confidence and — I should say — well-being.

Well it might be. The headmaster of that school was turning down potential entrants on the grounds that it would break his rule that no class should have more than 18 pupils (the average in a Danish state school is about 25), and his pupils are more likely to go to university than the average state school child.

The schools are not bastions of privilege. Denmark is an intensely democratic country: the royal family send their children to one of these independent schools, as do many of the senior figures of all the political parties, whether of the Left or the Right. The last factor ensures the schools a future whatever party comes to power. But many of the schools have a policy of not turning anyone away on grounds of poverty. Indeed, until recent cuts, the state would fund families to send their children to such schools as a matter of social equity.

And if the northern school I chose to visit first was academic in its orientation, I went to another in which there were only fifty pupils and which was more — what can one say? — holistic in its approach. Here the headmaster told me that he was especially concerned that children's education be practical; that the children learn through their hands; that they discuss things thoroughly. It was in sharp contrast to the other.

The parents had started the school ten years before, but it had recently moved into a new building. A core group had done most of the finishing work of the new building, had run out of steam somewhat and left it partly unfinished. There had been innumerable rows about what sort of school they were supposed to be running. I think that some of the more 'straight' parents had been at odds with some of the more 'hippy' parents. Also, there lurked some questions as to the political orientation of the teaching: the teachers were young and largely of the Left; not all the parents agreed.

There was no television, and no computer. It was an easy-going school attended distinctively (and Satish Kumar and his small school at Hartland have the same experience) by children whose parents have two distinct motives for switching from the state system. There were those whose views dictated finding an alternative sort of school; and there were those driven to it by their children's experience of state schools. On the whole, and usefully, the latter were the more 'ordinary' children and families. Thus, in Denmark, and perhaps anywhere, alternative schools are made more 'normal' by the attendance at them of children for whose parents they are a second and enforced choice.

Doubtless an intriguing tract could be written about how it came about that as Denmark discovered and developed universal adult suffrage it also became more, not less, respectful of the rights of individuals to dissent or differ from the emerging national consensus. In America, the need for a powerful consensus probably flowed from the need to 'launder' — to homogenise — vastly varied ethnic groups into a national identity. In Britain, we seem to have developed a powerful desire for the state to provide services on a basis of equality for all, without — at the time — being able to spot the hidden prices we would pay for the ideal: the abrogation of an individual's responsibility, and the sometimes dreary uniformity of the institutions the state would develop.

Historically the division between the state schools and the private schools is not so important as their common tradition. Both were strongly influenced by the educational convictions of a Lutheran clergyman, Nikolaj Frederik Severin Grundtvig (1783-1872), whose nationalism (in Denmark, this took then, and even now still takes, the form of an egalitarian pastoralism) was combined with a sense that the industrial, mechanical world was dangerous to the human spirit. In schooling, he particularly worried that the rote-learning of some schools was sterile, and the overall bias too scholastic, to stand the people of Denmark in good stead. He seems to have been right: in 1881, it was found that 43 per cent of the conscripts for the army who had been through the village schools could not read or write.

He thought that the coming of universal education

(introduced in Denmark in 1814) merely meant that the educational tradition deemed suitable for the elite and the scholastic would now be foisted on to the 'folk', for whom it would be useless.

He disliked the idea of an 'academic' culture and suggested instead a 'popular' culture, rooted deep in the people's sense of identity and traditions. He suggested the foundation of folk high schools, whose descendants are the modern state schools in Denmark, in which the country's and the people's own traditions and values would be celebrated.

But these were essentially adult schools: Grundtvig's greatest contribution to educational thinking was that adults should go to school, for periods ranging from a week or two right up to a year at a time, and learn whatever they felt they needed to become spiritually and democratically active individuals and citizens. He believed that people should pay something toward their adult education. He had learned his enthusiasm for adults learning from adults, especially by sharing accommodation and being in each other's company in a collegiate atmosphere, from visits to Trinity College, Cambridge. It was the English medieval university tradition which struck him as providing the model for a true people's education in Denmark.

Oddly, he had been impressed by a quite different aspect of university education from the strictly academic one which still dominates English educational practice: it was not the scholastic excellence which attracted him so much as the autonomy of the students in their learning.

It was a follower of Grundtvig's, Kristen Kold, who first founded 'free' schools, which in turn became the modern private schools. So private schools are not a mirror image of or reaction to the state system: they share and enshrine some of its most potent inspirations. Right from the start parents were free in Denmark to keep their children at home, or arrange an education for them in any way they chose, provided it met with certain criteria. So education in Denmark never achieved the status of a monopoly; nor did the private schools start or become defined as a rejection of the state system.

So the Danes have an educational system which allows and encourages greater diversity than does the British. It enshrines the principle of lifetime education. Parents are asked to turn out to elect a parent council to run aspects of both the private and folk schools. The children at either are legally entitled, but not required, to elect similar councils.

Anyway, the Danes did not develop in the same way as the British. And we now are ready, I hazard, to take a leaf from their book. The problem of persuading our Parliament that we should nationally be funding independent schools is, crucially, that we do not trust, and perhaps have badly damaged, the consensus in our society, and that we are terrified of losing it altogether. We live with the anxiety of the National Front, or the Socialist Workers' Party, or fundamentalist Muslims, or Rastafarians, or hippy communes, or the Rotarians, setting up schools with a dangerously narrow ethos and purpose. In a divided society, the argument goes, there would be a rash of schools devoted to preserving and ossifying the factions which already run the risk of destroying our national coherence.

Actually, this need not be a major problem. We already operate a system of sanctions — rarely but effectively used — by which an adverse report from Her Majesty's Inspectors of Education can result in a school being prosecuted for not fulfilling certain educational standards, or indulging in propaganda. The case law would presumably grow and develop if there were flourishing independent schools.

At the moment the lower size limit for a Danish private school is 20 (28 in the case of a school with a seven-year age span): there has been discussion about raising it to 45. The reason is that it has proved financially very hard to provide enough teachers to a school of less than 50 pupils. But there has also been a feeling that such a limit would preclude anyone setting up a school on what one government publication called 'passing discontent with' some aspect of state educational provision in a neighbourhood.

We would probably face an argument from the Left that education is not something one should pay for, and that the State has no business in encouraging a system in which education is in part a purchasable commodity. Some right-wingers might argue that the state has no business funding hippy adventures.

To these arguments, one can reply that they would seem ludicrous to the Danes. In an argument which is undoubtedly circular, one could claim that in Denmark a stout independent sector in education is not a result of the national consensus, but in part the cause of it. I believe that an Independent Schools Bill could go a long way toward providing a rallying ground for communities to discover that in their diversity there was much common agreement, across divisions of income, inclination, and racial origin.

After all, in Denmark we see a system in which quite poor people send their children to fee-paying schools; where parents of widely differing kinds co-operate — bumpily at times — in running their children's school; in which no new government dares to try to stamp out independent schools of whose ethos it disapproves; in which discipline and discussion can flourish together.

The heart of what I want to say about the Danish experience is that the business of coming together to fund and run small schools, the necessary compromises involved, the essential co-operativeness required, the rather high-minded pragmatism it betokens, are all exactly the sort of enterprise that the British — I mean, me and my neighbours in Hackney and for all I know, you and yours — probably both badly need and could hugely enjoy.

As *The Economist* has pointed out, independent small

schools are as necessary in Hackney as in Hampstead, in Kennington as in Kensington. The act of building such a school would demonstrate that English men and women, whether their grandparents were born in Bombay, Brixton, Barbados or Berkshire, could build a community around the shared enterprise of actively providing for their children's education.

CHAPTER SIX

The Issue of Size

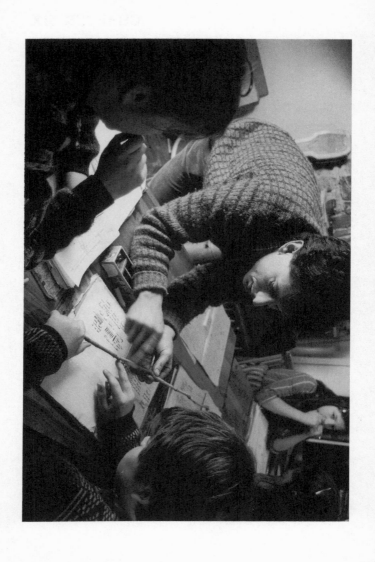

The Issue
of Size

THE OFFICIAL VIEW

THE PROFESSIONAL educational establishment likes
big schools. The citizen who pays its salaries and whose
children are the school system's real customers prefers small
ones.

However, the educational establishment does not
merely prefer large schools; it believes, very powerfully and
as a prime article of faith, that small schools cannot work. It
dismisses small schools — of which actually it has very
many, and will have more and more — as not 'educationally
viable'.

The clearest and most important statements of this
faith are to be found in the Government's White Paper
Better Schools which on matters to do with the size of schools
largely reflects the long-term view taken by the educational
establishment, and not merely the views of this Government. The Government view is supported by the ideas
within H.M.I. (Her Majesty's Inspectorate), a force which
in effect scrutinises the performance of schools, and which,
though working within the Department of Education and
Science, prides itself on its independence of mind.

The paper starts, obviously enough, with considerations about what schools should set out to achieve. It says
the purposes of learning are:

"(1) to help pupils to develop lively, enquiring minds, the ability to question and argue rationally and to apply themselves to tasks, and physical skills;

(2) to help pupils to acquire understanding, knowledge and skills relevant to adult life and employment in a fast-changing world;

(3) to help pupils to use language and number effectively;

(4) to help pupils to develop personal moral values, respect for religious values, and tolerance of other races, religions and ways of life;

(5) to help pupils to understand the world in which they live, and the interdependence of individuals, groups and nations;

(6) to help pupils to appreciate human achievements and aspirations."

An unexceptional list of requirements, though a bit short on old-fashioned written culture — literature and history, for instance. Still, noble and useful enough for practical purposes.

The paper then goes on to talk a little about the curriculum which such a set of principles would imply. It does not question, hardly states, and absolutely assumes that a curriculum is a series of subject compartments which will be taught to a group of children gathered together by reason of their having been born in the same year. The teachers of children over the age of eleven will be as near to specialists in one of these subject compartments as is possible. Certainly, there is an explicit assumption that it is the nature of the curriculum which determines how many teachers a school will need.

The argument looks, at first blush, impeccable, but it rules out any sympathy for small schools, which — by definition — cannot 'deliver' the curriculum most of us have grown used to assuming 'should' be taught.

The curricular machine begins in low gear at the primary stage. "Although the curriculum which the primary schools seek to deliver is largely a common one, they use widely differing language to describe it. . . The Government believes that there is wide agreement that the content of the primary curriculum should, in substance, make it possible for the primary phase to . . . place substantial emphasis on achieving competence in the use of language. . . on achieving competence in mathematics. . . introduce pupils to science. . . lay the foundation of understanding in religious education, history and geography, and the nature and values of British society; introduce pupils to a range of activities in the arts; provide opportunities throughout the curriculum for craft and practical work leading up to some experience of design and technology and of solving problems; provide moral education, physical education and health education; introduce pupils to the nature and use in school and in society of new technology; give pupils some insight into the adult world, including how people earn their living."

This is beginning to sound a daunting prospectus, and it is worth remembering that in a primary school, most of this work would be accomplished by one teacher. The primary school remains mostly a school with generalist teachers.

The curriculum, thus far, should be possible for most primary schools, says the White Paper. But: "The main constraints lie in the number of teachers and their collective qualifications and skills, and in the size of the school. The smaller the school, the more serious these constraints are likely to be."

The curriculum the White Paper has discussed thus far is reasonable in scope and intention. But hidden within it is the germ of specialisation, not so much of the children as of the teachers. While most of us would probably think that a group of children should not be taught for several hours a day by just one person, and that a well-balanced education will probably require that children meet different kinds of adult minds during their day, in these paragraphs we see a quite different development: we see the school establishment beginning to assume that such a broad curriculum — so many 'subjects' to be covered — will require several teachers to deliver it.

Importantly, we see the curriculum as the object and purpose of the school. Where its demands require large size, there is no mention of competing values which require small size. Though the document allows that some factors may require that a small school stays open, this is a matter of regret, because of its implications about the curriculum.

Moreover, the curriculum is seen as having breadth, but its depth is not discussed. Thus, a school needs to be big enough to deliver the whole of the curriculum. But a small school is not seen as having the specific advantages of, say, allowing a family atmosphere whose advantages might be believed — by some or many of us — to be worth the sacrifice of a little restriction in some areas of educational activity.

The idea of the curriculum-driven school intensifies with the coming of puberty and the transition from primary to secondary schooling. Again, the Government's view looks extremely reasonable. It even resists the introduction of the full curricular rigour of specialisation at too young an age.

"In the Government's view, older pupils in the primary phase should begin to be systematically introduced to teaching by members of staff with expertise in an area of the curriculum other than that which the class teacher can offer. Moreover, while it is important in the secondary phase to secure a match between the teachers' subject qualifications and experience and the teaching programme, there are advantages in not exposing the youngest secondary pupils immediately to the full range of individual specialist teaching."

In the early years of secondary schooling, all the pupils are to undertake the same programme, including language, science, mathematics, physical and religious education, humanities, geography, history, art, music and drama, home economics and C.D.T. (craft, design and technology). One foreign language, and then two, should be on offer. In the fourth and fifth years, children can begin to specialise, and to drop their weak subjects or those which won't be much use to them.

And there we have it. A smooth transition from the one teacher, one class, world of the primary school to a world replete with many subjects, which will necessarily require many teachers in any institution which can properly deliver the curriculum which is their home.

In the paragraphs which state policy in the matter of size, "good education" demands that "each school should as far as possible be kept large enough to justify sufficient teachers to provide all pupils with a curriculum which measures up to the principles set out [above]." Small schools may sometimes be necessary, but they will be expensive (presumably because of the necessity of providing more teachers per pupil in order to provide the breadth of qualifications and experience the curriculum requires). Geography, and the need to allow religious freedom, may require such exceptional expenditure.

The upshot is that a primary school ought not to fall below a roll of 100 pupils and three teachers. An 11–16 school will need at least six forms of entry (meaning that six classes of thirty pupils each will join each year), and an 11–18 school will need a sixth form of 150 if it is to be viable. The smallest comprehensive without a sixth form would need a population of at least 900, on this argument.

Once the assumption that a school must be curriculum-driven is in place, cost considerations flow from it perfectly, especially when pupil numbers are falling, as they are for secondary pupils now. There will be between 15 and 20 per cent fewer secondary pupils in 1991 than there are in 1986. That implies the equivalent of 1,000 secondary schools standing empty (even granted that L.E.A.s are dragging their feet about making changes to the number of class-rooms they operate).

The Audit Commission (the independent adviser to the House of Commons on the management of public funds) believes that the shrinking rolls means that in that period we could save between half and nearly three-quarters of a million pounds a year by the end of the decade, or could spend it within the education system more effectively. If we do not close schools and rationalise the system, the argument goes, that money will be squandered in teaching empty desks.

The Commission looked at the problem in their *Towards Better Management of Secondary Education*, which concentrates on the role which a different approach to managing secondary teachers might play during the period of falling rolls. "Teachers are a precious resource," it says, having already noted that the quarter of a million teachers we have cost around £3 billion a year, and that the falling roll of secondary pupils represents a £1,000-per-teacher opportunity for non-teaching cost savings (such as in heating and so on).

We need, says the Commission, to make sure that "teaching resources are not wasted. Within the limits of appropriate group sizes for particular subjects, empty seats in any class represent a wasted opportunity for a teacher to impart knowledge and enthusiasm for a subject. As school rolls fall, the waste entailed by empty seats will become more serious unless schools are reorganised on a scale which has hitherto proved impossible."

Instead of rationalising, many authorities are keeping schools open, and incurring a heavy cost in doing so. They are especially forgoing the opportunity to participate fully in proposed government schemes such as technical and vocational training, and the new ideas about integrating pupils with special needs into the general system.

"More important, the funds wasted on teaching empty chairs and maintaining, heating and cleaning redundant classrooms will not be available to improve teachers' relative pay and to enhance the educational facilities, books and equipment as well as the curriculum available to pupils. Teaching costs account for 68 per cent of the total annual cost of secondary education of (on average) £1,139 per pupil. Since central grant support of the order of £450–600 per pupil (depending on the authority) is based on the number of pupils on school rolls, it follows that if no action is taken to reorganise local school systems, L.E.A.s will face an uncomfortable choice between placing extra burdens on the local ratepayers, curtailing the curriculum or 'penny-pinching' on maintenance, books and equipment."

Putting this very crudely: the Commission reminds authorities that the Government pays them a per-pupil rate (it could hardly do otherwise) and not a per-school rate. So herd the pupils together in as small a number of schools as possible, the better and cheaper to keep them warm and to deliver the curriculum. These are the economies of scale.

The Commission notes that it has no business commenting on how much Central Government decides to spend on education (though it notes that Central Government has shifted the burden of providing education expenditure towards the local authorities). It outlines three options which L.E.A.s could follow:

a) maintain the existing number of schools and teachers, and endeavour to maintain the current curriculum, inevitably at vastly increased unit costs (costs per pupil); or

b) reduce the number of schools and teachers at a rate which maintains current curricula with reduced total expenditure and unit costs kept at current levels; or

c) maintain the existing number of schools but reduce the number of teachers in line with falling school rolls, at once impoverishing the curriculum and failing to take advantage of the cost savings which capacity rationalisation would bring.

"The Commission favours the adoption of the second position as far as possible: the first is wasteful in terms of scarce teaching skills (since group sizes will be unduly small) and the costs of heating, cleaning and maintaining school buildings. And the third is an unnecessary worsening of provision."

But, the Commission laments, L.E.A.s are not taking the sensible course: they are not letting teachers go or organising them into bigger schools.

Instead, each pupil is on the receiving end of more and more money: an increase per pupil, in real terms (i.e. taking account of inflation) of 18.6 per cent.

Much of this increase occurs because the pupil-teacher ratio (P.T.R.) is falling. In other words, in most schools, there are fewer pupils per teacher. This would strike most people as a rather good thing but actually, the role of the P.T.R. can be almost as pernicious as that of the curriculum if it is enshrined at the price of good teaching.

The Commission believes that because the P.T.R. has been improving over the past few years, and because its value has been overstated, some authorities are congratulating themselves on having achieved a lower P.T.R., and ignoring the fact that there seems to be no direct link between the quality of education a child receives and the P.T.R. within which he is taught. Indeed, the Commission believes that within a band of plus or minus 20 per cent,

P.T.R. has no proven relationship to quality of education: in other words, you need vast classes or tiny ones before you can begin to say that size of class makes any definite and predictable difference to the quality of a child's education.

This adds up to an argument to suggest that big classes may not necessarily be the enormous problem they were once thought to be.

In any case, in the conventional wisdom, we have an argument in favour of a large curriculum delivered by specialist teachers to small classes, of which the Commission dares to challenge only the last prong. It suggests the L.E.A.s are sheltering behind the 'improving' P.T.R.s that smaller and falling rolls bring. In the Commission's hands, this becomes an argument in favour of departing from the P.T.R. as a sole indicator of good schooling, and presumably allowing instead a rationalising of small, low-P.T.R. schools into rather fewer higher-P.T.R. schools in which there are sufficient teachers to deliver the 'full' curriculum.

Oddly, one might turn this on its head and suggest instead that one could discard the present P.T.R.s, and allow larger classes within schools which would otherwise close. A small school — or one with a falling roll — might flourish if it were allowed to depart from some cherished P.T.R. which had been falsely enshrined.

Inflexible P.T.R.-led management has, the Commission says, produced the situation where some schools are supplied with teachers rather arbitrarily, and perhaps extravagantly, simply because, for instance, the number of pupils rises fractionally in one year: a P.T.R. threshold is crossed, and another teacher appears.

The Commission usefully points out some other criteria which might be used to manage the resources of a school. One is that it should be subjected to an analysis of curriculum-led staffing, in which a certain curriculum is agreed for the school, and then a staffing requirement outlined. The result, says the Commission, is a series of constructive debates and negotiations, but L.E.A.s tend to find unacceptable the unpleasant realisation that the full curriculum combined with limited teacher numbers tends to imply high P.T.R.s. They return to P.T.R. as their favourite indicator, though it means squeezing every other resource they have at their disposal, such as book provision.

The Commission notices one surprising anomaly. It finds that "a teacher in I.L.E.A. (Inner London Education Authority) teaches an average 5.2 fewer lessons per week than a teacher in the Isle of Wight (assuming a forty-period week)." This is the contact ratio: the proportion of timetabled time the teacher spends in class. The Commission suggests that a 2 per cent increase in the contact ratio of the average teacher would result in a saving of nearly 6,000 teachers, or £72 million.

But the system is full of rigidities, as the modern jargon has it. Change is resisted.

The Commission says that it is discussing the situation in terms the Government sets. "Clearly, with different curricular assumptions, the economies of scale will be different. The view of the Government, expressed in *Better Schools*, and that of H.M.I., is that it is educationally disadvantageous for comprehensive secondary schools to have fewer than six forms of entry which is equivalent to 900 pupils for a school serving pupils aged 11-16 and appreciably more than that for 11-18-year-olds.

"Thus economic considerations and professional educational judgements alike point to a need for school systems to be reorganised to avoid schools below the six-forms-of-entry threshold. In January 1985, D.E.S. statistics show that about 1,790 comprehensive schools out of a total of 4,382 had fewer than 800 pupils. Although some of these will not be catering for the full 11-16 age range it seems certain that a very large number of schools will be too small to be viable educationally. The situation is certain to worsen since . . . school over-capacity is going to increase. An alternative approach open to an authority is to go against the professional views of the Inspectorate and others and respond to demands that schools should be deliberately made small with the aim of maintaining communities on a more human scale. The extent of the required narrowing of the curriculum could be illustrated by curriculum models. Such models would not however show the disadvantages of the wide variations in ability within classes which are an inevitable features of small schools."

There we have it. Large classes, an inability to deliver the widest curriculum, mixed ability classes, all combine with cost to make small schools 'unviable'.

CHAPTER SEVEN

The Research

The
Research

WE HAVE looked a little at the issue of how the smallness of schools is perceived by Government: inherently inefficient educationally, and expensive budgetarily.

We turn now to what the facts are about the size of schools and their actual performance.

But it is notoriously hard, and perhaps impossible, to assess a school's performance. To tot up examination results would be some sort of an exercise, and given perfect distribution of bright and dim children through the school system might demonstrate how well the various schools had performed in transforming talent into information properly or correctly delivered on a given day. But perhaps those schools with good examination results will have achieved good scores by ignoring the less bright (whose non-scoring would be outshone by the fabulous scores of the achievers). Perhaps the children at the school weren't happy, or emotionally developed. Perhaps they were implanted with information, but had developed no spark of dissidence, or of spiritual life, or of practical capability.

In any case, brightness is not perfectly scattered through the system. For too long, of course, 'socially deprived' neighbourhoods have been indulged in their educational failure: but surely, even given that indulgence, they do have special difficulties.

It is inherently hard to set goals for a school career. Initiative, adaptability, the development of skills — 'life skills', entrepreneurship, citizenship — are not qualities one can easily measure. Nor are the qualities of affection, community identity, or the development of a sense of responsibility in children.

It would be quite wrong to say that the educational establishment is blind to the need for these less tangible qualities. It constantly and rightly lays emphasis on them. Nor would it be fair to say that the present school system — even its big schools — never helps children achieve them.

We can, however, safely say two things. They matter a great deal. One is that, search as one may, there is no evidence that big schools perform better, academically, than small ones. And there is some evidence that small schools are happier places than many large ones.

The best review of the findings of various researchers is to be found in *The Rural Community and the Small School*, edited by Diane Forsythe. It only adds up to 'case unproven' as to the measureable quality of small-school education.

Unfortunately for the crude arguments in favour of small schools, it also finds the evidence inconclusive there. One of these is that children suffer from being bussed from their villages to a nearby town: the evidence suggests not, though there have been cases of unpleasant bullying on school buses. Another is that communities suffer if their schools are taken from them: again, the evidence is inconclusive. Clearly, most people would prefer that their child walk to school a comfortably short distance; similarly, many of us like the idea of communities with a school at their midst. But we will not, it seems, get much comfort from the sociologists when we assert these prejudices.

It is hardly surprising, however, that there is a good deal of evidence that parents who are free to choose, choose small schools rather often. This last choice is not always based on the smallness of the school. It is often based on the narrow academic performance of the school, on some element of cache, or just a school's reputation for turning out children who seem to do all right.

But then, parents who choose the schools their children attend normally have to pay for the privilege: they tend to 'buy' schools which are small, have many good teachers, and achieve fairly high academic standards within a framework of discipline and family atmosphere.

Moreover, that sort of choice is mimicked by those lucky enough to be able to find such schools in the state sector. Size is not always the determinant. Quite often, it will be a matter of choosing the school which has a reputation for academic success or for success in turning out well-behaved young adults. The latter of these objectives may not excite some educators, but it enthrals parents.

Yet those schools within the state system which are most envied and most sought after are almost all below the size which is educationally viable, according to the official view.

The state system has a range of relationships with schools ('controlled', 'aided' and 'special agreement') in the voluntary sector. The average sizes of these schools in 1984 was well below the magic 900 we have seen already to have become enshrined. The aided schools averaged 744, and the controlled 858. Even county schools only averaged 925 (and falling).

It is easy to suggest that these small schools perform well and are admired because they are fortunate: they have managed to appropriate towards themselves special sources of funding and expertise, or had a conveniently advantaged catchment area.

However, disadvantage in the wider neighbourhood is

not by any means an infallible indicator of school failure.
H.M.I. in their *Aspects of Secondary Education in England*,
looked at the broad spectrum of schools. Under the heading
of 'Pupils' Behaviour — Some Special Problems' they
looked at a sample of schools which reported social
difficulties, and others which declared themselves mostly
free of them. H.M.I. found some severe problems, such as
vandalism and indiscipline, but also found them to be very
limited and limited to few schools. These schools seemed to
be large or fairly small about in proportion to the general
population of schools. Most were in poor neighbourhoods.
Out of 25 such schools, one was small and one was rural.

Importantly, they found good schools in surprising
places.

H.M.I. identified a sample of schools under the
heading, 'Schools Notably Free of Problems'. "The first
example is of a school serving a notably poor and difficult
area known to have many special problems. Vandalism and
violence were commonplace in the neighbourhood and
other schools in the area faced high rates of truancy and
absence. Yet this school, an 11-16 mixed comprehensive
still in the process of reorganisation from a secondary
modern school, had virtually none of these problems. One
of its most obvious strengths was the high quality of concern
for the pupils, backed by an effective structure of pastoral
care which had been established by clear analysis and
discussion of the needs and by careful planning. Communications were good and arrangements sufficiently flexible to allow members of staff to use them as occasion
required. The school, like many others, had not solved all
its curricular problems, but classroom relationships were
such that pupils made a willing response and showed good
attitudes to work. Their general confidence and pleasant
ease of behaviour were impressive. The school had encouraged an extensive programme of extracurricular activities in
which many pupils and a high proportion of its staff took

The Research · 91

part; it also made the most of its good fortune in having a residential centre in Wales, where groups of pupils were given opportunities to learn from living together and sharing responsibilities."

We are not told the size of that school: it might have been vast. But it is a comfort — so far as the argument of this book is concerned — to note the following problem-free school.

"The second example is that of a mixed 11-16 school of just under 600 pupils, which at the time of the survey had recently evolved from secondary modern to comprehensive school and community college, with the comprehensive intake by then in the fouth year. Reorganisation, coupled with strenuous efforts on the part of the headmaster and the local authority advisers, had helped this small rural school to attract some very well qualified teachers. Positive and succesful efforts were being made to adapt curriculum and staff to the changed nature of the school, both the younger teachers and their more experienced and established colleagues working well together. A great deal of effort was put into defining and establishing pastoral responsibilities, and into seing that work was pitched to the needs of individual pupils. In many of the classes responsive learning was being encouraged through wide reading and excellent provision of both books and other resources. A good programme of out of class activities, involving a variety of responsibilities for the pupils, coupled with 'linked courses', served to extend the experience which pupils brought to their learning."

Two more schools are noted as being especially good. One of them was a large school, of nearly 1,100 pupils.

Overall, "the earlier accounts of schools in serious difficulty point to a strong association with adverse environmental and social factors, but the converse does not necessarily apply."

H.M.I. reminds us that poor neighbourhoods may have many strengths. Even if 20 per cent of a school is composed of slow learners, that may not make it a problem-ridden school. H.M.I. suggests that there may be a threshold of disadvantage (of difficulties combined with inadequacy of resources) which tips the balance.

But the survey tells us mostly that there is no single factor that makes for a bad or good school. There is certainly no single policy which could be imposed which would create a good school. This matters when size is suggested as exactly such a criterion. It also matters when it is suggested that a poor neighbourhood could not be expected to manage to produce a good school.

The more we find that no single authority or inspiration can claim a monopoly of wisdom on schooling, the more we also surely find we can make an argument in favour of allowing full rein to diversity within the system. Certainly there is no reason why a small school should not succeed, in spite of the doctrine that no small school can be 'educationally viable'. And those small schools might just as well be in towns as in the country.

Between 17 and 19 May 1983, H.M.I. visited Walpole Cross Keys County Primary School in Norfolk. This was a school of 46 pupils in two classes aged 5–11. There were three classrooms, "two of which operate as a single unit by means of a sliding partition . . . a corridor is used by both classes for a variety of purposes and the office which is shared by the head and his secretary is also used on occasion as a workspace by pupils." There was a field for soccer, netball, athletics and rounders. A cesspit had contaminated the sandpit so it wasn't in use at the time. The school was made "attractive by varied displays of pupils' work. It is, on the whole, imaginatively and resourcefully used, well maintained and the quality of caretaking is good."

"The school is reasonably well resourced for all aspects of the curriculum. There has been some funding by the local authority for specific items of equipment; parents have helped with raising money for books, a language centre and a computer." There is a head and a full-time teacher; both spend time on in-service courses; a music teacher spends a little time in the school. The youngest 16 are in one class. The remaining 30 are in another. Each class is taught by its class teacher. "The teachers are enthusiastic and hard working and take a keen interest in the children's needs and welfare . . . Considerable attention is given to developing oral language and communication skills. The total environment includes a wide range of items to provoke interest and discussion. Local and national visits extend the children's experience and provide material for discussion and inquiry. Effective relationships within the school encourage interchange of ideas and parental involvement ensures that children communicate with a range of adults. Stories of good quality are read to both classes. The children are articulate and can readily explain current activities to visitors.

"Language guidelines are presently being considered and, over a period of time, it is intended that a range of additional material will be introduced to supplement the main reading scheme now in use. At all stages, the children are well motivated and read with interest, understanding and enthusiasm . . . The school might profitably consider ways in which practical experience and play activity might be further used as a basis for introducing reading skills. Children are gradually acquainted with higher reading skills and learn to use reference material with confidence. They turn readily to books for pleasure and information . . .

"At all stages, children write about a range of experience and appropriately record activities within home and school."

The encomium continues, through environmental studies, music, physical education (sometimes using other schools' facilities), and religious studies (including assemblies with spontaneous prayers offered by the children).

"There are excellent relationships betwen staff and pupils . . . Parental involvement in the life of the school has been actively encouraged . . . This is a happy and purposeful school characterised by profitable co-operation between pupils, staff and parents."

This is surely the kind of schooling people dream of. It was taking place in a school which had a third of the numbers of pupils recommended as a minimum generally. By any normal consideration it should have been three times bigger in order to achieve 'educational viability'.

I had been steered toward the H.M.I. report for Walpole Cross Keys by one of its fans. For a comparison with another small school I turned to one for Burston Primary School, also in Norfolk. It was chosen because Burston has such a famous reputation as the place where parents once were highly involved in helping a pair of rebel teachers start and run their own local school, in what became known as the Burston School Rebellion. That school is now defunct, but remains a powerful symbol of what a poor village could achieve.

Burston was inspected in 1983. The school caters for children aged 5–11. The school had 48 children and three full-time teachers; a music teacher came in once a week. The teachers went away to training courses.

The report is slightly more critical than that for Walpole Cross Keys and yet it is positive for all that. But we see some of the difficulties which attend small schools, at least potentially. The three teachers stuck to their class groups, as is usual with primary schools: why not expose the children to varied teaching staffs, implies the report. The younger children deal with too rigid a timetable. The reading of the six-year-olds seems to have been a little poor; but the standard soon improved. In mathematics, "there are instances in which the work is not well matched to the needs of the children and where the emphasis on the formal skills precedes the understanding to be gained through initial and

necessary practical experience." The art work seems to have
been a little uninspiring. The school was congratulated on
"its attempts to introduce science to this age group of
children" . . . but . . . "perhaps this is the time to
re-emphasise the objectives of the course with a view to
emphasising the investigative approach to science using the
very rich opportunities offered by the village environment."
In history and geography there was too much copying and
note-taking, but "the children enjoy and are well informed
about both subjects."

The conclusion is that this is a school characterised by
"disciplined, sound learning in which the pupils develop
personal and social confidence and sufficient confidence in
basic skills to proceed to the next stage of their education".
The criticisms when they come are that the curriculum,
though wide, is "rather narrowly conceived as the learning
of facts". The community and the environment and more
autonomous studying would help. "The pupils are well
behaved and polite. During the inspection they were eager
and sufficiently self-confident to discuss with strangers not
only their work but also the application and general
significance of what they were doing."

Burston was one of several schools which the inspectors
discussed — this time not by name – in their *Education
Provision and Response in Some Norfolk Schools.* Norfolk is
famously rural: but a third of its people live in three
principal urban areas. The county spends £3 million
bussing secondary–age children to school. It has about the
usual spread of 'classes' (professsions, trades and manual
workers) as the rest of the country. The position of the
schools is very varied. In one primary school there is a
P.T.R. of 31:1; in another, 27:1. Of its 458 primary
schools, 152 have fewer than 60 pupils on roll (218 have
outside lavatories), and 42 of them have 30 pupils or fewer.
In some of these small schools, there is only one full-time
teacher and perhaps the equivalent of another 0.6 of a

full-timer in part-time help. "Although a very small primary school may appear to have a favourable P.T.R., the actual number of teachers may nevertheless leave it unable to provide a broad curriculum," says H.M.I.

In one small school, "the stock of musical instruments was limited to a collection of untuned percussion instruments contained in a single, small cardboard box." Small schools had difficulty in physical education, especially indoor activity. But in general, in primary education, smallness of size did not seem a major preoccupation.

Of course, H.M.I. always reminds us of the prevailing doctrine about size, and then provides evidence to contradict it: "It is difficult for . . . small schools, with only two or three staff and limited resources, to provide curricula of breadth and intellectual stimulation but to their great credit some were managing to do so. One first school with fewer than 30 pupils had a broad and interesting curriculum with carefully designed links between its component parts, but in another school (with fewer than 50 pupils) there were no overall guidelines for any subject and there was, perhaps not surprisingly, no evidence of any exploitation of the inter-relationships between for example elements of religious education, geography, art and craft, and history."

Small schools are presented as creating specific difficulties: they demand a low P.T.R. if there is to be a sufficient blend of teaching skills and qualifications in the school; they may soak up teachers which the rest of the system needs. But they perform as the rest of the school system does: in this school well; in that school less well.

CHAPTER EIGHT

The New Style of Education

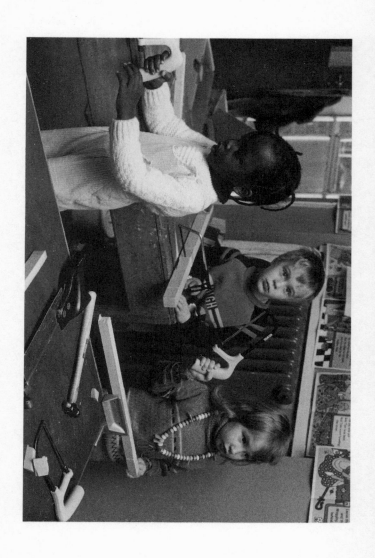

The New Style of Education

THERE IS a very good children's book by Russell Hoban in which a small boy keeps outwitting a professional team of sportsmen because, whilst they are highly skilled at the formal and complex games they have perfected, he is even better at the self-same activities. Only he did not know that the games had complicated rules and required skills. He had thought that what he was doing was 'mucking about', at which he excelled.

I do not think that school can just be a matter of mucking about. But there are signs that schools are beginning to be given a really strong message that practicality is just as creative as 'free expression'. The engineer is as creative as the poet; the inventive is as exhilarating as the artistic.

The Royal Society of Arts ('founded in 1754 for the encouragement of Arts, Manufactures and Commerce') has been sponsoring Education for Capability. It is deliberately intended to encourage schools to develop lines of thought which reach beyond 'academic' education. One of Education for Capability's founders, Sir Toby Weaver, a former senior D.E.S. official, has written that in part this idea of capability incorporates sensitivity, and appreciation of things of beauty.

He goes on: "The art of living is concerned with the formulation and solution of problems, with doing, making, designing and organising, with productive, constructive and creative activity of all kinds. By contrast the educational system is inbred, of little relevance to living of life outside it.

"The standard curricula of schools, colleges and universities, with their emphasis on acquisition, through mainly passive methods of pedagogy, of propositional knowledge, are too little concerned with helping people to become competent, to cope, to develop their creative capacities. These personal, problem-solving and organising skills (life skills as they are sometimes called — and they are needed not least by the academically able) cannot be taught by chalk and talk; they involve the students in learning what *they themselves* regard as relevant, by a process of trial and error under the guidance of those who are themselves appropriately skilled; and their achievement cannot be assessed and certified by written examinations as we know them."

He then stresses that what a person can do is more important than what he knows. This is in line with increasing calls from industry and elsewhere that certificates of capability, stressing what a person can do, might be more useful than examination results which suggest a certain amount of knowledge in, say, geography. It is a line of argument which has been met by recent moves in some examinations to continuous assessment (though this carries further problems of assessment of a pupil by a quite possibly biased educator).

This sort of thinking in education has resulted in programmes such as 'Problem Solving: Science and Technology in Primary Schools' promoted by the Engineering Council and the Standing Conference on Schools' Science and Technology. It is intended to develop ways in which young children can get a hands-on scientific education, in which making, organising, communicating are important.

We have seen the degree to which the sacredness of the curriculum can powerfully determine educational systems. Curiously, the engineers see the way a problem-solving technique is precisely cross-curricular as one of its great merits. It teaches flexibility of mind, rather than compartmentalisation.

The brochure which launched the project stressed that the kind of work it wanted to see would "encourage creativity and inventiveness in designing and making three-dimensional working artefacts which achieve a given task; cause pupils to learn or reinforce some science and perhaps mathematics by experiencing concepts relating to energy, materials and their properties, structures, forces, speed, measurement, accuracy, consistency, stability and control; give opportunities to develop manipulative skills with simple tools and a range of materials; develop communications skills within and between teams and adults, including drawing and display of ideas and achievements; involve some elements of planning and organisation."

Put like that, the ambition seems laudable but perhaps a little high-flown.

But I was enormously impressed — and did not expect to be — by a visit to the near-derelict site of a vandalised state school in Croydon at which Stuart Sexton hopes to see a new private, pro-technology primary school rise, phoenix-like.

Mr Sexton is a chemist and a politician. He enjoys science and Conservatism. He enjoys the idea of diversity in the school system, and does not think that it is impossible to deliver to parents some sort of education credits which they must use for the good of their children.

When he hears that people are worried that there might be almost too much experimentation under this system, he is inclined to say that there will have to be mistakes, but there are mistakes made every day anyway.

The sort of parents who might rally round such a figure would be, I think, a little predictable. In Croydon, they would largely be the rather strait-laced and thrusting bureaucrats and technocrats who are, perhaps, a little too concerned to see that their children should 'get on', in some rather over- and narrowly-defined way.

And my heart sank rather when I heard that the proposed school would be dedicatedly technological. I though, well, what about the poetry and whimsicality? We can't all be production managers, even if it is true that we have rather few of them at present.

But come the Saturday of the open day at which Mr Sexton and his team were to show off the sort of thing they admired, and much of this was dispelled.

The most important thing one detected was that technology did not mean anything too bleakly or narrowly numerical. Instead, it all looked remarkably like mucking about. There was a small presence there from British School Technology, demonstrating the sort of thing that primary school children can come up with given a steer in the right direction.

There were gizmos of every kind for every sort of thing. Bridges in various sorts of Lego, of course. But better than that, things which were not made from 'kit' items but which had been conjured from the raw materials themselves.

Two or three simple tricks and devices were on display. First, a glue and cardboard system for making strong right-angle joints. Enormously simple, but giving the chance to make box structures of immense strength to five- and six-year-olds.

Then, a very simple device for making wheels and pulleys. Just neatly-cut plastic wheels which would snap together to become very fat (to work with drive belts of elastic bands), and with an easy punch to make axles.

Another fundamental problem solved.

Box structures and wheels: the making of engines, houses, boats, bridges, robots, vehicles. Engineering and architecture delivered to small hands.

Suddenly, one saw that a three-dimensional, working, robust machine-making world was opened up. No need here for woodworking skills, or for the workshop environment, or for dangerous tools, or for greater strength than a child has. No need for all the clumping about with heavy tools which seems tiresome to many girls. Limitless possibilities, the chance of easy success, and small cost.

The enchantment of this is that creativity, art, science, making, and doing — in short, mucking about — can be offered as they should be, freely and in a way which offers something to every skill level: not intimidating the shy, but not constraining the successful.

This was a project for primary schools. As the young progress, they face the world of work more directly. The present Government has been working on putting work-oriented training into the hands of more and more of them. This directly vocational and training role in schools and beyond can be criticised on the grounds that it does not meet the highest scholastic goals, namely that the individual's mind be stretched and honed, with no reference to its utility, especially not its social utility or its utility to the world of work, employers and exploitation.

We see now, I think, that this purity of approach merely meant that we turned out many children from schools who were neither equipped for success in the world of work, nor articulate enough to be successful dissidents, nor personally well enough developed to be happy beneficiaries of the enforced idleness of unemployment. They certainly weren't self-starting entrepreneurs, many of them.

So training the less able of them for the world of work would be likely to succeed in one of two or three ways. First, they might be more able to get a job. Secondly, they might get a taste for learning. Thirdly, they might gain confidence that they were not education-proof.

Fourthly, one might say: no learning is ever wasted. Nor are its results predictable. One might have intended providing education to enable a child to get work, but the grip of a technical skill, once put into that person's hands, could blossom into inventing hospital equipment or terrorist bombs. All education, even work-centred education, must be offered on trust and in the optimistic expectation, usually fulfilled, that people will put it to work, more or less, for society.

We have not begun to explore the relationship between the world of the child and the world of the adult. In future, this will not be so much the world of school or of employment; or of pupil or employee. We are likely to see a state of affairs in which neither the child nor the adult is put into a ghetto determined by others. Some children will work, and some adults will be schooled.

Further, a child's education, and the budget society gives him or her, may well in future be capable of being spent in a garage or shop, not in exchange for goods and services, but for instruction.

One sees the signs of this already. Some local radio stations are staffed in part by young people who work there free, and hope one day to get a job, but meanwhile take the dole. Many children of businesses get a flying start by working alongside adults in them. Marks and Spencer often employ schoolchildren at quite responsible work: showing them what excellence is like and how to begin to operate in an environment where courtesy and high standards are normal. More controversially, one sees the same thing in MacDonald's, where young people, often from poor neighbourhoods, work in the nearby burger bar: there are those who call this exploitation, but it is just as easy to see it as the means by which a certain slickness, a certain pride in efficiency, can be transmitted.

Just as modern technology is bringing the world of work into the home, as increasing numbers of people find they can be quite easily equipped to do at least parts of their work amongst their family, so the world of work will increasingly receive children in its midst. Naturally, there are limits to the intermingling in either direction: but we have not begun to discover them yet.

The educational system, spurred on by an impatient government, is having to adjust fast to a whole series of new 'initiatives' which have come, it seems, not out of the educational establishment, but from employment ministers dedicated to the enterprise culture. Projects such as the Technical and Vocational Education Initiative (T.V.E.I.), Non-Advanced Further Education (N.A.F.E.), the Youth Training Scheme (Y.T.S.), and the Business and Technician Education Council (B.T.E.C.) are all determined to blur the distinction between education and training, and to suit pupils for work.

There seems to be some confusion between the roles of the Departments of Education and Employment, whose Manpower Services Commision is working with educationalists to promote T.V.E.I. There may even be some anxious competition between them for supremacy at the interface of the schools and the training programmes.

It is too easy to say that the educational system is being 'balkanised' by these various strategies: but in the midst of the confusion it is possible to suggest that, what with sixth form colleges, open techs (to match the Open University), city technology colleges, and so on and on, the existence of diversity within what is supposed to be a unified system is becoming very obvious and might as well be admitted.

More than that, we are losing the academic bias in education. A few years ago this would have sounded like a contradiction in terms. Now it is a recognition that educating a population for life is more complicated than reading them stale lecture notes on the Thirty Years War.

At the 1987 National Association for the Support of the Small School conference, Mike Davies, one of the heads of an enormous comprehensive in Milton Keynes, described how his school was learning how to dissolve itself into smaller units, and intended to run as many of its operations as possible at a team level of 150 pupils and a small group of teachers. He said that the school had been invited to consider what its future development ought to be. The staff decided that one of the things they would like to see would be the buying-in of time and space in neighbouring firms.

Mr Davies did not think such a thing was likely to happen, even in so explorative an environment as Milton Keynes. Yet what could be more obvious?

What could be more likely to answer the demand for young people who understand business? *The Economist* (December 20, 1986) devoted several pages to the problem of training for work, and identified the peculiar disjunction between education and the world of work as a major hazard facing the country.

The Economist's analysis compared experience overseas; especially it pointed out that British firms do not devote much time and energy to training their young staff, or indeed their staff of any age.

The paper pointed out that in many other countries, firms see themselves as in various degrees part of the education process.

These are all arguments which will encourage the Human Scale Movement, which likes to stress emotional and manual qualities as being as important as intellectual ones. They all imply that schools as delivery systems for a formal curriculum may be barking up the wrong tree as a matter of intention, and that to shape the institution of the school so as to fulfil its curriculum-delivery role may endanger its ability to be a place where really useful capability learning can take place.

But more positively yet, the kind of thinking described

here clears the way for all sorts of new initiatives to grow up, uninhibited by counter-movements which suggest that only the traditional, state-owned school can manage.

Kim Taylor's *Resources For Learning* demonstrated very forcefully that in the past and in other countries there have been and are approaches to education which marry up the experimental, the practical and the freeing of children from being dependent on teachers. He lists the rural Swedes with their correspondence courses and summer schools; the Americans with their assignment system; the Russians with their pioneer palaces. The Swedish child with a course he or she follows through the post; the American embarking on a tailor-made task; the Russian child attending school in the morning, but in the afternoon going to a sort of activity centre, are all demonstrating that the teacher-standing-and-teaching is not the only way to learn.

Mr Taylor points out that the ideas of the Victorian Charlotte Mason, developed for home-bound girls of middle- and upper-class Britain, led to the correspondence courses still used by many isolated families. Charlotte Mason above all espoused the idea that it was the book itself, the writer of the book, which was vital to the young reader. She told the governesses using her system to speak very briefly about the book, and mostly just to suggest what it had meant to her. Then get the child to read it just once, and to explain back some aspect of it. The one reading was important, she thought; and so was the retailing of the experience.

Charlotte Mason was dealing with governesses and books. No television, radio, video, film, accessible libraries, tape recording, computers, easy travel. Yet she had seen the basics of a child's finding his or her own way around material.

Now, devising extension courses which can be used by parents and children, teachers and children, children and children, will clearly be tolerably easy, and relatively cheap.

They could be used in schools or out of them. They can be highly technological or not. Designed for groups of children or for loners.

However, if we deploy the idea of extension learning as something desirable in itself, we will need an increasing certainty that children will master the rudiments of reading, writing and arithmetic. As many children as possible need to be equipped with the basic skills which will see them capable of doing much of the future exploring for themselves. This may mean that at primary school children do slightly less creative work and more acquiring of basic skills.

At the other end of the scale, the freer children come to be from schools, the more it is likely that they will need other sorts of establishments which will provide either the physical equipment or the challenging minds, or both, that a home, neighbourhood or small school environment cannot provide. Sweden and Denmark have summer schools for this sort of purpose; the Russian pioneer palaces would also serve as a model. Further education colleges, the Open University's summer schools and others all provide models for this sort of activity. All of them, and especially tertiary or sixth form colleges, would make it easier for the middle rung of a child's education to be away from school; with the 'A' Level standard catered for more formally.

Of course, a skills-centred approach might also suggest that once a child had mastered certain basic skills, he or she would be much freer to cease education. It is time to accept that there is no virtue whatever in undergoing the process of education in itself. The passive endurance of n hours of a teacher's exposition on this or that subject is not in itself improving to the child or the world. In fact, it might well be that the greatest single incentive for children to learn the essential basics that so many now escape would be to say that the child is free to leave off education only once they are assimilated — but as soon as they are assimilated. It is likely that what most blocks most young adults from being attentive to their schooling is that they have not mastered the elementary skills which make it enjoyable: give them an incentive to master the basics, and one probably has found the key to their becoming eager pupils later on.

But we must have the courage to accept that it does not matter if in mid– or late adolescence a person prefers working in a factory or a milk round to being in school or learning. Adolescence is not the best time in which to study: it is fundamentally too restless a period. For many and perhaps most people, it will be better to achieve certain basic skills and then to try one's hand at a job of some sort. The higher reaches of learning can come later, if need be, or if desired.

CHAPTER NINE
The Political Environment

The Political
Environment

TO BEGIN with the good news, it is worth noting that the laws which regulate education are very much more flexible than at first sight seems likely. First, there is no law that a child must attend a school of any kind. A child must only be in the position of receiving a 'full-time education' appropriate to his 'age, ability and aptitude'; this can be 'at school, or otherwise'.

Many parents have taken advantage of this 'or otherwise' to keep their children at home. Some of them have run into the difficulty that their child is registered formally at a school and that the arrangements for a child to be de-registered may be tricky. But even here the difficulties are not insuperable, and, well-handled, most education authorities seem to realise that they have little to gain by making difficulties which would have scant chance of succeeding at law.

However, a parent who takes a child out of school will not usually receive much help in doing so, and certainly no financial or major resource help; equally, he or she will not be allowed a rebate on whatever proportion of his or her tax bill goes to schooling.

It is only a small step from an individual family keeping

a child out of conventional school to wanting to join with others to start a school. Historically, churches have done this, and operate schools which are funded by the state in greater or lesser degree. At one point, they provided the majority of schools.

It is not outlandish to suggest that this practice should be extended to groups of parents or to communities.

The most important campaign now, then, is to redefine the way in which schools are funded so that it is easier for parents and others to start schools, or to club together in an educative way which they may refuse to call a school.

One way of signalling the change would be to fund parents and pupils as they seek education, rather than to fund the institutions which provide it.

The present Conservative Government has gone some way toward this by expanding slightly the channels which already existed whereby it could help fee-paying schools to accept pupils whose parents could not afford fees.

And the Government has invented the idea of city technology colleges (C.T.C.s), which it sees as schools at which science and technology will be especially nurtured for pupils who have demonstrated considerable and special motivation to learn. The Government claims that these will not be schools at which only an intellectual elite will be taught: commitment will matter more.

The Government is hoping that 20 of these colleges will be in place quite quickly, but it wants to see around three-quarters of the money for them coming from industry and others. As this is written (in March, 1987), there is some doubt that industry is prepared to co-operate in a venture whose overtones have seemed political rather than purely educational. In crude terms, C.T.C.s may turn out to be bad P.R.

The C.T.C. has grown out of a desire in this Conservative Government to redress what it sees as a long-term and disabling tendency to favour the generalist and the academic children and style of education, at the expense of the technological and engineering skills which, it believes, would better help the country to compete industrially.

The idea goes rather further than this, though. The C.T.C.s look remarkably like the sort of project which Stuart Sexton was trying to promote when he was the special adviser (a political appointment) to Sir Keith Joseph as Secretary of State for Education and who lost his job there when Kenneth Baker took over as Secretary of State.

Of the two C.T.C.s likeliest to get off the ground, both are schemes which Mr Sexton in part initiated. One, in Solihull, has been taken over by the Hanson Trust, an aggressively successful firm which can use the Government's new rules on charitable giving to offset against tax the million pounds over five years it intends to spend on the project. There is also some hope that a C.T.C. will be started at Liverpool.

Mr Sexton's idea was that it is possible to create independent schools in which there would be an unabashed pursuit of excellence for pupils of every ability. He also believes that it is possible to introduce children to modern technology very early in their school careers; that a traditionally Christian and disciplined school life is a great thing; and that governments should make it easier to start such schools, probably at the request of a private trust backed by industry, foundations and individuals. He has in fact gone ahead and started just such a private and fee-paying school in Croydon, in the Tory heartland, and though it is at present a primary-only establishment, he has hopes of expanding it. In March, 1987, it had fourteen pupils, all five or under, but is set to grow(see pp103-5).

The ideal of independent schools, founded by parents and heavily backed by them, but funded by the state, could easily grow from this kind of movement. Mr Sexton is already an enthusiast for the various channels by which governments can fund diversity of education.

Developing the theme will require more than persuading governments to fund pupils on a per head basis and as individuals, rather than funding the school as a whole, though this will be difficult enough. It will be a question of developing a means of funding loans on capital equipment, such as houses, redundant schools and so on, so that new schools can be started.

There will be much resistance to these ideas, and they almost certainly will not come about as a smooth progression.

The Conservative Government in May, 1987 announced that it was going to make it easier for existing schools to opt out of the present local government sponsored system. What matters now will be whether they will allow a new breed of school, or education club, to start up from scratch.

The Government will not necessarily enjoy seeing its moves toward technology colleges, nor its sympathy for fee-paying schools, nor its preparedness to fund independent schools, developed by others as a rationale for state-funded schools with a very different ethos.

Governments will say that every move toward a freer system will take the country closer to a situation in which any eccentric minority may set up schools catering to its whims, and that these may be very poor educationally and very dangerous to a society seeking consensus within diversity.

Actually, however, the State already has laws at its disposal which lay down extremes of bad practice and prejudice which put a school outside the law. But it is likely to find great difficulty in accepting that the best response to the present uncertainty about what constitutes a proper education and what is the best institutional framework for achieving it is to be more open to experimentation, rather than less so.

In fact, it will be necessary to remind the Government that the mere fact that any school it funds could be required to be a local school, and may even have obligations placed on it to be open to any local child fulfilling certain requirements, would have a powerfully consensual effect on possible schools. It is unlikely that any deeply eccentric school could attract the breadth of local support such a school would need, and could be legally defined as needing, to be considered for state funding. After all, who will send their child to a school which fails to turn out competent and successful children?

But we are entering a period in which it will have to be faced that the essentially authoritarian model of school, one which matched an authoritarian society, is now redundant.

Schools were tolerably successful in turning out obedient citizens who were well-drilled for the fulfilment of a lifetime's wage-slavery in which too much imagination would have been a dangerous thing in many people.

However we have moved into an era, which will probably develop and intensify now that it has arrived, in which all the obvious buzz-words have come to have some real substance: we need 'self-starters'; we need entre-preneurs and enablers; we need lateral thinkers. We need armies of creative people who are problem-solvers. We have not the smallest idea what this country will be famous for making or doing ten or twenty years from now. The names of what we will mostly be making or doing have probably not yet been invented. The likelihood is that even those as yet unnamed and unknown goods and services will be replaced shortly after we have got used to them.

About all we know of the future is that it will require a great deal of adaptability. What is more, we can be sure that whatever it is we decide to try to make or do, there will be other nations all around the world with similiar skills and just as much determination to ply them for reward. The Third World, which once gave the rich world a sort of working class to deal with and exploit, is rapidly approaching an economic enfranchisement which it will tax our ingenuity to match.

In such a world, it is terrible nonsense to say that our people will not need to be disciplined: of course they will be. They will need to be talented, informed, cultured by turns and to differing degrees, of course. But obedience to a master or to a class-ideal will not likely be required of them. Subservience is a depreciating asset.

Nor are the new needs confined to the creation of wealth. The idea of a proficient and strong professional class being well or tolerably paid to administer skills and services to their inferiors is declining. The Welfare State, as a delivery system of services to the inadequate, is likely to undergo rather thorough overhaul as people choose to buy certain services, or do them for themselves, wherever possible, and rely on the state only for certain emergencies or exigencies. This could, of course, have very ugly consequences for the State's hospitals, schools and social security offices.

It will reqire a great deal of ingenuity to make sure that the essential minimum which remains really is acceptable, and better than anything we now have.

All the same, we have reached a point in the social development of most affluent nations where it is both possible and necessary for most people to be encouraged and equipped to perform for themselves many tasks which they had thought to be the preserve of the 'middle class', or people with some special professional skill.

The present Government has initiated a good many new schemes with the intention of helping young people to bridge the worlds of school and work. So we are in the interesting position of seeing the state school system wanting to consider different approaches — to do with helping children develop problem-solving skills, and towards developing the capacity to pursue their own project work — which will progressively take them toward accepting that the formal school system may not be the sole or best custodian of the modern education of children.

Fiercely defensive of its reputation, the modern school system will have to accept, modestly, that it was only slightly successful at achieving the task it set itself, and that the task itself is largely redundant. It wanted to deliver academics, of whom we have scant need; and failed.

The way is open, not for casual experimentation, but for a multitude of approaches conducted by people who are dedicated and seriously committed. We need to be respectful of the fact that we are dealing with the life-chances of children. But we do not serve them so well, nor is the present system so free of experimentation, that we need be too cautious of a radical approach.

The idea of state-funded independent schools is, potentially, attractive to people of any position in the modern political spectrum of the country. One can see support for it amongst Socialists, Conservatives and Social Democrats.

Certainly, however, amongst the Socialists, there is no evidence that the idea has yet appealed to anyone who is listened to by party managers, but that could change very rapidly.

The latest Labour thinking is represented by *Equality and Quality* (Fabian Pamphlet 514), which is not party policy in itself, but is written by the party's Shadow Education Minister, Giles Radice. Its thrust is not favourable to independent schools (though there is a nod in the direction of special help for community schools): indeed, the assisted places scheme (under which the Government funds scholarship places at fee-paying schools for the poor but bright students) would be done away with under Labour.

Mervyn Benford, one of the most important champions of the small school, is part of the S.D.P. educational policy team, whilst Stuart Sexton was an advisor to Sir Keith Joseph when he was Education Minister. Both are educational 'radicals', but each is very different from the other. However, the education debate is one in which it will pay people to find as much common ground as they can with one another: it is one in which the old Left-Right political spectrum runs the risk of dividing people whose interests are common.

It is Mr Sexton, in particular, who has done the most work on the governmental changes that would be needed to allow the State to fund independent schools. In this, he is in line with a good deal of thinking which is coming from the Tory side of politics (see Suggested Reading). It is a particularly Tory inclination to see all monopolies as potentially dangerous, and the state education monopoly of education for the less well-off as no exception. He sees the existing system whereby the Government can fund 'voluntary' schools as one which could be built on.

Meanwhile, on the radical wing of the Conservative Party, there are propagandists for a more thorough-going reform on Sexton-esque lines.

The 'No Turning Back' group of Tory MPs produced a pamphlet in 1986 (*Save Our Schools*) which argued that the most profound reform of the educational system which has been mooted — the voucher system — would face such opposition and be so dramatic, and probably chaotic, in its effect, that it would be wiser to look for other reforms which would achieve desired, but not undesired, effects.

Under the voucher system, a child's parents would be free to 'cash in' a voucher anywhere in the state or private systems. However, it is felt that there would be such a gadarene rush for the good schools, and little immediate mechanism for reforming the bad ones, from such an overnight change that the system could not stand the strain.

Instead, the group proposed that a series of reforms would do the trick with less chaos. First, schools should be turned over to strengthened boards of governors with the power to hire and fire, to set curricula, and to manage the school budget, which would be handed over direct from the Government on a per capita basis, with perhaps some room for exceptional weighting for schools in particular circumstances.

This proposal would weaken the L.E.A.s, and very probably the teachers' unions (because there would be a powerful incentive for schools to strike individual deals with their staffs).

The group also argued for a Danish-model system whereby new schools could be started by groups of parents in a community. It argued that the state could match capital funding on a one-for-one basis.

These were temperate and useful suggestions, fairly carefully put, allowing for the rhetoric about left-wing propaganda and so on which many Conservatives believe to be rampant in our schools. (Truth to tell, even a right-winger should comfort himself when anything rampant takes place in school: tedium is the greater enemy).

A less temperate, more thorough-going, and at times much more suspect proposal has also emerged from the Hillgate group, which includes Lawrence Norcross (a London comprehensive headmaster) and Roger Scruton (a philosopher and journalist). This group stresses the need for a traditional education, which it explicitly believes should be modelled on the sort of schooling intended by the Butler Education Act of 1944, and which 'moderns' and 'progressives' have overthrown.

Egalitarianism, left-wing propaganda and the loss of the good old 'hard' subjects in favour of 'soft' ones are diagnosed as being part of the egalitarian thrust, which also includes the erosion of the examination system.

Thus, though their pamphlet is called *Whose Schools? A Radical Manifesto*, its thinking is extremely traditional. This will reassure many potential parent-readers that here is a programme which would return the schools to exactly the kind of educational system which has, in fact, over the past half-century and more created a society which dislikes enterprise and ignored the potential for capability and creativity.

However, it is also a manifesto for the sorts of institutional reforms which would produce independent schools. It shares the widespread demand for the schools to be freed from L.E.A.s and be vested in trusts; it wants the Government to extend the city colleges concept. However, it stresses the need for a national curriculum, which carries with it the threat of over-prescription by the central state, and the concomitant erosion of exactly the variety and choice which we need to encourage.

S.D.P. thinking, as expressed by Dr David Owen in November 1986, is to scorn the Conservatives' city technology college scheme as being too rapidly and forcefully imposed on the current system, and being too obviously a way of creating schools which snub and ignore the L.E.A.s.

However, he too saw the sense of a government building on the voluntary state school funding which was set up in 1944 as a base from which greater variety, and perhaps especially technological excellence, might be achieved. He also suggested that money might be put aside for intensive science courses at universities and elsewhere for secondary school students who were suffering deprivation at school.

There was a hint here that the S.D.P. might look kindly at a system under which independent schools could be helped into existence, provided that the L.E.A.s could be brought to agree with them.

It seems very likely that any party or combination of parties which is likely to gain power could find a way through the political dilemmas which encouraging diversity will involve.

However, promoters of human scale education will face

the problem of double-think. For instance, the present Secretary of State for Education, Mr Kenneth Baker, has said, in Parliament, "I have visited many village schools with small numbers of children in them — 15, 20 or 30. They provide excellent education. I wish to make it clear that it is not the Government's intention to close such schools. In many cases they provide an essential ingredient to hold a community together." (*Hansard*, October 28, 1986)

Actually, there is very little evidence that villages much notice the closure of the small schools in their midst, at least in the sense that people move away because of it. We should argue for small schools not merely because of their community utility, but — more powerfully — because their customers want them, and because they are the sorts of institutions which can become growth points of personal, and only then of community, well-being.

But Mr Baker's enthusiasm in any case needs to be seen against the background of *Better Schools*, which, though it was the product of Sir Keith Joseph's reforms, has been endorsed by Mr Baker in his circular *Providing for Quality: The Pattern of Organisation to Age 19*, published in May, 1987.

In it, there is no serious sign that the thinking which is changing the schooling of older children — its practicality, especially — is being thought through for the younger pupil. If it were, there would be plenty of room for small schools, the positive encouragement of volunteers and more widespread consideration of giving the budgets of all schools to their governing bodies.

All the old anxieties about small schools are re-expressed in this latest circular. The educational establishment seems prepared to trundle on, with the occasional rhetorical snippet thrown in to appease the electorate's taste for smallness.

Indeed, the group which wants to start any sort of

school, which will have, of course, to start small, will face a sophisticated apparatus of official prejudice against smallness.

Several counties have initiated investigations into the state of their small schools, and in the case of some of them, for instance Suffolk, the reader is left in no doubt that for most small schools closure is the preferred solution of the authority. Others take the view that small schools are inherently fraught with managerial and budgetary problems, but that sharing facilities, and a flexible view on staffing levels, can help maintain the viability of some.

Almost all the rural counties have come up with initiatives to try to improve the lot of small schools. Yet in the present climate of lack of confidence amongst many educators, a small school which was loudly defended — and positively supported, day-to-day, by its community — could probably stave off closure. Often this will come down to volunteer activity, in teaching, fundraising and maintenance.

It is noticeable, however, that the politicians are discussing changes of a quite limited kind in the school system. The Tories would like to foster independent, but mostly traditional, schools; they would like to see a more goal-oriented and practical education. In both of these main thrusts they go further than their rivals, and in directions which chime fairly with some of the themes of this book.

But they are not yet exploring the teacher-free school, nor the possibility that whilst schooling may become lifelong, it may become less obligatory upon the young. There is nothing in the current political discussion about extension learning for teenagers, or about summer schools for the more intensive learning they cannot do at a small school or at home. There is nothing yet about the idea that a neighbourhood, or a house, may be as effective a place to learn as a school.

None of this matters too much. It will not be

politicians, who must deal in mass movements, who make innovations. That has always been for the philanthropic and the peculiar.

Appendices

APPENDIX 1

Ten Beauty Tips
for Small Schools*

Professor E. C. Wragg, Exeter University

THE ONE major consolation about a contracting education system is that many people, raised in the larger schools of the expanding 1960s, suddenly discover that small can be beautiful once they come to terms with falling numbers. Elizabeth Taylor will tell you, however, as she copes with a few falling rolls of her own, that staying beautiful is hard work.

Small schools, located principally in rural and inner city areas, have been under direct or indirect attack for some time. It was inevitable, when birth cohorts dropped dramatically from well over 800,000 a year during the mid 1960s to below 600,000 during the later 1970s, that these schools would feel the pinch and that their very viability would be challenged. During the 1980s small schools have had teachers taken away from them, have had their real funds reduced, have occasionally been subjected to abuse from local politicians, and have sometimes been closed down.

---

* This article is reproduced with the permission of the Head Teachers Review, published by the National Association of Head Teachers, in which it first appeared in Spring, 1985.

Yet in many local authorities small primary schools are not only alive and well but are the standard form of school. Particularly in rural counties schools with between two and five teachers can even be in a majority. Furthermore the H.M.I. Primary Survey pointed out that small schools were often particularly good at utilising their environment, though the children were less likely to visit museums and some of the other features available to city children.

Many of the present day issues in education pose considerable dilemmas for small schools. Eric Bolton's speech in May 1984 about the need for more specialised teaching to raise standards was greeted with dismay in two–teacher schools. I suppose the answer would be for one teacher to be the expert on maths, science, technology, media studies, health education and environmental studies, and the other on everything else. That should make each teacher worth a salary of about £25,000 a year for a start, so it will be greeted ecstatically in Burnham circles.

The next problem is that of teacher assessment. Will the two teachers assess each other? And if only one is given a merit payment, will they stop talking to each other and insist on separate staff rooms? Relationships are crucial in small schools, and the major problems tend to occur when three teachers who do not get on together come into conflict and have nowhere else to turn, or when children and parents lose respect for one or more teachers in a closely knit community from which there is no refuge.

I can see some of the possible negative points about small schools, but it was because I support the many examples of good practice that I wrote to the *Times* last year pointing out the plight of schools under threat. I sometimes teach in a two-teacher village school myself, and so I offer these ten tips for staying beautiful on a take-it-or-leave-it basis, not because they say anything new or from any sense of arrogance, just from affection for what can be done well on a small scale.

1. Mobilise parents

Parents are the backbone of many small schools, helping out with transport, running jumble sales and fetes, and leading fierce support if the school is threatened. Any small school which alienates its parents does not stand a chance. Yet parents can also be a powerful political force, since they are usually both ratepayers and voters.

I remember talking to a senior civil servant about cabinet ministers he had worked with. What frightened them to death, he confided, was not members of the Opposition hurling abuse during debates, that was all part of the fun, nor was it mass petitions or attacks in the press. Apparently the most effective way of sending political giants into a neurotic frenzy is to write a well argued personal letter saying something like, "Me and my friends at the Bridge Club are so concerned at your failure to do *X* that we shall not now be voting for you in the next election." What turned the tide, when local politicians tried to take away teachers from most small schools in Devon, was 2,000 personal letters written to county council leaders quite spontaneously by parents, and the sight of over a thousand of them outside County Hall for a crucial County Council meeting.

Parents also have a distinguished record now of helping in the classroom. Many schools encourage them to hear their own children read at home and then come into school to work with other pupils, always, of course, under the direct supervision of a qualified teacher. There is a wealth of talent amongst parents, even in the most unlikely circumstances. In small inner-city multicultural schools it is especially vital to win the active support of parents for their children's learning, because they can feel alienated if they are left out.

2. Enlist politicians

Although some politicians have attacked small schools, many recognise that it is an emotive issue. Indeed there are strong supporters of village schools in places like the House of Lords, many of whom live in rural areas. At local level there is the M.P., and usually certain councillors will make it part of their political work on a County or District Council to advocate the continued support of small schools. But they must be identified and briefed, otherwise they feel foolish in debates if they do not have all the necessary information to hand.

Amongst the most important local politicians are the Chaiman and Vice-Chairman of the Education Committee or any key members of the Schools Sub-Committee whose decisions are often rubber stamped by the full Education Committee or County Council. In Metropolitan areas crucial allies can be councillors in wards where there is rehousing taking place, because it is here that small city schools need powerful allies.

Should a school be threatened with closure then it is most important that the politicians should have all the facts. In one village the two teachers and the children's parents went round the whole area finding out how many parents of children under five would be sending them to the village school during the next few years. They then invited local politicians to come to the school, almost always a good move, because it is much harder for people to be stone-hearted about places they have actually seen. Not only did they fill the classroom with work by the present generation of children, but they also diplayed photographs of every child in the school as well as of the under-fives whose parents had promised to use the school. It was no contest. The school was reprieved and is now thriving.

3. Encourage community use

With millions unemployed and many more retiring early, community use of educational premises is highly desirable. In some places the school is the only building of any size and is used extensively, but in others it stands empty outside weekdays from nine till four. Although there can be tension between schools and adult users of premises, these can be resolved by goodwill. If evening and weekend youth club activities cause damage, for example, a word with the club leader should help, and if that fails a joint committee can be set up to look into grievances.

In the United States many schools that were under threat, when enrolments began to plummet, found themselves rescued by strong voices in a grateful community. Local people certainly appreciate being able to use a school for their own leisure and recreation activities, and there can be tangible gains for the school. One rural middle school that became designated 'community centre' found that pressure from adult users soon brought in extra furniture and equipment and led to a notable increase in its facilities for drama.

4. Federate

Federation of small schools can lend considerable strength to all of them as well as allowing them to preserve their individuality. It must, however, be handled and resourced properly. If a federation of five, ten or 15 small schools is to work properly then teachers must sink any petty rivalry and jealousy and concentrate on the greater good.

A well organised federation should offer the following educational possibilities:
(a) joint in-service days for teachers
(b) curriculum expertise (Eric Bolton will be delighted if the schools between them can rustle up knowledgeable teachers in major areas to enthuse their colleagues)
(c) job swaps for a term or a year between teachers within

the federation giving professional renewal and a change
of scenery
(d) shared bus trips to places of interest
(e) both inter-school sports (especially small-sided games,
like five or six a side) and regional teams (often a small
school cannot field a full 11 or 15, but a region can)
One other form of federation is also worthy of note. In
some areas they have formed federations of parent-teacher
associations or governors of small schools. These can also be
a powerful combined force.

5. Mobilise facilities

We are used to mobile libraries and travelling shops and
ice-cream vans, but there is still very limited use of mobile
educational facilities. Yet both Bedfordshire and Devon
have successfully launched a technology bus idea, which
houses the latest equipment for children to be able to come
aboard and study micro-electronics under a peripatetic
specialist teacher, and Hereford and Worcestershire uses a
bus laden with micro-computers for similar travelling work.

Although the initial outlay can be high the returns are
good. The bus will be extensively used, and it will certainly
be cheaper than replicating specialist facilities all over the
area. It should not be used as a substitute for proper
provision of educational equipment but rather as a supplement. A mobile bus can also be multi-purpose: technology,
books, video, sports, the arts. There is no reason why it
should not be built on a flexible model.

6. Look and reach out

One major line of attack against small schools is that they
can be inward–looking, self-contained, smug and self-
satisfied even, and that they are therefore set in their ways
and unable to change. There is no reason, other than their
intimacy, why they should be any more complacent than

any other institution, but it can be a danger so steps must be taken.

One possibility is to approach local authorities and providers such as teachers' centres, colleges and universities, to put on special in-service one day and half day courses for teachers in small schools. It is easy for people to assume that all in-service provision is equally applicable to all teachers, but a course with emphasis on taking a wide view of some particular issue but relevant to teachers in small schools is what is needed. It is also important for teachers and heads to attend regional and national conferences. Those in small schools often have to give way to colleagues in larger schools when the favoured names are drawn up, but is a principle worth fighting for. Indeed when those in authority are drawing up some committee or delegation containing the usual mix of interests and making sure there is a balance of north and south, men and women, ethnic minorities and special interest groups, someone must call out "what about the small schools?"

7. Seek sponsorship

I like to think that a maintained system of education will endow schools with what they need, but the reality of financial cutbacks is that sponsorship of one kind or another must be sought. Parent-teacher associations are the usual benign sponsors, but if Harvey Smith can ride a Sanyo Music Centre rather than a horse, and if electronics giants can sponsor football teams why shouldn't local businesses and firms offer occasional nuggets to schools on a much more modest basis? It is not unknown for individual or business sponsors to provide sports kit, equipment or other bounties in return for nothing more than an acknowledgement.

8. Innovate

It is tempting in a small school to muddle along pursuing

what is safe so that one is immune from criticism. Yet one of the most exciting events in any school is the innovation, not earth-shattering perhaps, which captures the imagination of children, teachers and parents. I have piloted both the B.B.C. Junior Microelectronics course and the B.B.C. Domesday Project in Clyst St. George Primary School, a two-teacher school near Exeter, because the Head is a firm believer in the need for innovation, experiment and risk-taking alongside all the solidly valuable bread and butter teaching. The children love exploring innovative ideas.

9. Use school broadcasts

This leads me to my next point, the use of schools radio and television. We cannot possibly keep up to date in every field and good quality radio and television programmes extend every school's horizon. Yet some teachers merely glance at the annual programme, resolve to take 'Watch', 'Zigzag' or whatever other annual favourite they have, and fail to notice excellent programmes like 'In the News' on radio, or the many first-rate science and technology programmes. Have a detailed look at your B.B.C. and I.B.A. annual programmes. You will be astonished at the range. They offer a treasure trove to teachers in small schools. Nor should correspondence courses be ignored. Although most are not aimed at younger pupils the correspondence course is an ideal way of providing something requested by only one or two pupils.

10. Publicise what you do

Some heads are strongly against any regular contact with news media on the grounds that reporters will do mschief to the news or sensationalise it. This is an understandable but mistaken view, especially since the advent of local radio. If the mass media are not given good news to report they will write nothing about education until something goes wrong. Then the public wrongly assumes that schools are full of violence and vandalism. It is an important quality of senior managers of schools that they know how to handle local media. Let the local newspapers and radio know about the many exciting events taking place by sending them a well written, concise single page of A4 once in a while. They are often sick of yet another report of the Women's Institute Marmalade Sale, and only too delighted to write about school events. In these hard times small schools need all the friends they can get, and there are no better ones than the public at large.

Manifesto:
Movement for
Education on a Human Scale

The need...as if people matter

Small is beautiful applies as urgently to education as to economics. Fritz Schumacher wanted a society 'as if people matter'. We need schools 'as if people matter'. Such schools have to be of human scale.

The loss of human scale

As recently as, say, thirty years ago, it was still common for small communities to have their own primary school and many had an all-age school. The all-age schools have gone and the received wisdom having been that rural primary schools should have at least three teachers, many villages no longer have a primary school. There are some survivals, some revivals, but the tendency has been, and still is in official circles, towards small school closures and amalgamations. This ignores the fact that young people generally prosper in small places.

The excuses: comprehensive education!

Small market towns used to have their own secondary schools and cities a range of schools of various sizes and types. These schools seemed to serve some sections of the population better than others and a proper determination to provide equality of opportunity for young people led to comprehensiveness...a principle we firmly support. But the route taken was that of the American High Schools with a broad range of subject choices for the widest range of abilities and interests rather than the alternative, more common in Europe, of a common core curriculum.

The result: giant size schools

This decision led to big size. The desire, at least at first, to retain 'streaming' and also the sixth form, with its complex combinations of specialisms, and the desire of teachers to have specialist facilities, reinforced the tendency to giantism. Schools of from 1,800 to 2,000 pupils were regarded as the optimum size for all-through comprehensives, 1,300 a minimum. Now 800 to 1,000 is considered a satisfactory minimum. Although many such smaller schools, especially in rural areas, have survived and prospered, the tendency has been to large numbers.

Appearances deceive

With bigger size, what is visible in school...buildings, facilities, the range of subjects, success at the top...becomes more impressive. But, as time has gone by, other effects of size have been felt such as bureaucracy, ill-discipline, and strained relations between teachers and children, between teachers and parents, and between the school and the community. Its negative influence also becomes visible from time to time in truancy, vandalism, violence...the behaviour only of a vehement minority, sensationalised in gossip and the media. More widespread and significant among the silent majority, is a feeling that much of schooling is marking time and can lead to a sense of personal insignificance and failure. Many young people, dismissing the school as an inflexible institution where they matter little and learn less, become altogether alienated from the values enshrined in the school.

Other factors inside and outside schools

All the ills of education of course cannot be attributed to size. The quality and morale of teachers, their training and re-training, the support and resources made available, the nature of the curriculum....these and other elements impinge upon the school. Nor are the children insulated from negative influences in their own families and in society at large. However, many urgent improvements now sought by teachers, administrators and parents are much easier to achieve when schools are small or subdivided into human-scale units.

The benefits of human scale

1. More personal contact with individual children becomes unavoidable and good relationships are more easily established. Education and welfare can be more naturally integrated, with the same adults teaching the children and caring for their general well-being.

2. A more active style of learning, increased group and independent learning (especially among older pupils) can be encouraged without elaborate structures of control.

3. Without the rigidities of an elaborate timetable, individuality in the content and rhythm of learning can be extended.

4. Education for social responsibility can start from a young age because pupils can be given a say in decisions affecting them or the whole school without resorting to cumbersome consultation procedures.

5. Small schools need to use parents and other adults in the community to supplement the teachers' work and to use community facilities to supplement their own. The consequence is a greater involvement of the children in the

community and a more natural 'real life' curriculum for them.

6. Parents have a real choice when there are several smaller schools.

7. A good standard of discipline is easier to establish and maintain. Because of increased contact and better relationships between adults and children, teachers have an improved opportunity to encourage good behaviour. Conversely children will be less inclined to misbehave in order to be noticed.

The education on a human scale movement

The Schumacher Society does not claim that large schools can be transformed into smaller ones, or larger units reorganised into smaller units overnight. But the time is ripe to reverse the trend towards large size. At the primary level, the resistance to closure is widespread. At the secondary level 'falling rolls' both increase the threat of closures and provide an opportunity to retain schools that have become substantially smaller.

Human scale a necessary but not sufficient condition

Small schools are particularly suited to many of the improvements sought by teachers and administrators such as active and experiential learning, community involvement with the school and school involvement with the community, 'education for capability', a core curriculum, forms of assessment based on achievement rather than on examinations, a negotiated curriculum, new approaches to the use of time, etc. Parents and other adults now tend to blame many of the problems of the school on 'size'...a simplification no doubt but one based on instinct and fundamentally sound. A human scale is not a sufficient condition but we believe it to be a necessary condition.

The challenge of education on a human scale

We challenge those notions of 'efficiency' and 'economy' which have been used to close small schools and to justify large ones. We believe that the loss of quality is too high a price to pay for such 'economy' and urge the following propositions.

1. That only exceptionally should village primary schools be closed against local and parental wishes.

2. That large schools wishing to sub-divide into federations of smaller units on a single site should be supported.

3. That existing secondary schools regarded as 'too small' (an increasing number as rolls decline) should not normally be closed and that ways should be explored for them to work co-operatively with other schools and to adopt practices and technologies that compensate for smaller size with supporting advice and services from the L.E.A.

4. The co-operative efforts by parents and others to restore small infant and primary schools to their villages should be considered sympathetically for assistance by L.E.A.s.

5. That as in other European countries, small community schools anxious to work within the state system should, wherever possible, be viewed sympathetically for funding by L.E.A.s and their progress and qualities evaluated as examples of good practice.

6. That studies of individual small schools within the United Kingdom and systems of smaller schools in other countries should be undertaken and publicised.

Human scale inside and beyond education

We intend to work in association with people already active in particular schools and in a wide range of organisations-...some directly educational, some not but holding compatible aims...to launch a movement to sustain, develop and inform an active and professional interest in 'education on a human scale'.

Suggested Reading

Perhaps the most forthright account of the prejudices for
and against the small school is contained in *The Rural
Community and the Small School*, edited by Diana Forsythe
(1983, Aberdeen University Press). I have glanced at the
more recent *The Small Rural Primary School*, by Adrian Bell
and Alan Sigsworth (1987, The Falmer Press), and thought
its tone a shade sociological. I am a frank admirer of L. C.
(Kim) Taylor's *Resources for Learning* (1971, Penguin and
out of print). *Education for Capability*, edited for the Royal
Society of Arts by Tyrrell Burgess (1986, National
Foundation for Educational Research/Thomas Nelson) is a
useful account of the new hope to put skills in the hands of
children, rather than information alone. Philip Toogood's
The Head's Tale (1984, Dialogue Publications) is an account
of his days as headmaster of an innovative comprehensive.

I received it too late for comment in the body of the
text, but I think that reformers of the present education
structure will probably find Stuart Sexton's Institute of
Economic Affairs pamphlet, *Our Schools – A Radical Policy*,
useful. It is available from I.E.A., 2 Lord North Street,
London, SW1P 3LB or from I.E.A., Education Unit,
Warlingham Park School, Chelsham Common,
Warlingham, Surrey, CR3 9PB.

In one of the most enlightened publications policies of
any government department, the reports of Her Majesty's
Inspectors, and much else, are available free on inquiry to
The Publications Dept., Department of Education and
Science, Honeypot Lane, Stanmore, Middlesex, HA7 1AZ.

Useful Addresses

- Exeter University School of Education runs a unit
  devoted to small school policy: Small Schools Network,
  University of Exeter School of Education, St Luke's,
  Exeter, EX1 2LU.

- The National Association for the Support of Small
  Schools is an invaluable pressure and support group: 91
  King Street, Norwich, NR1 1PH (0603 613088)

- The Institute of Economic Affairs now has an Education
  Unit which can be expected to produce a good deal on the
  policies the independent school movement needs to
  encourage. (See Suggested Reading)

- The Movement for Education on a Human Scale,
  Hartland, Bideford, North Devon